Splendid Soles

Photography by Amy Setter

Printed in the United States of America

First Printing, 2018

ISBN 978-1-62767-193-4

Versa Press, Inc

800-447-7829

www.versapress.com

CONTENTS

A DREAM THAT WAS ROME SOCKS

by Deborah Breland

FINISHED MEASUREMENTS

7 (8, 9, 10)" finished circumference; socks have negative ease and will stretch approximately 5". Finished length is adjustable

YARN

Knit Picks Hawthorne Kettle Dye (80% Superwash Fine Highland Wool, 20% Polyamide (Nylon); 357 yards/100g): Compass 26690, 1 (1, 2, 2) skein.

NEEDLES

US 1 (2.5mm) DPNs or two 24" circular needles for two circulars technique, or one 32" or longer circular needle for Magic Loop technique, or size to obtain gauge.

NOTIONS

Yarn Needle
Stitch Markers

GAUGE

30 sts and 44 rnds = 4" in St st in the rnd, blocked.

Notes:

These socks were loosely inspired by the imagery in the movie Gladiator. I loved all the scenes of Russell Crowe sweeping his arms over the tops of the golden wheat that grew on his land. The instep pattern and the seed stitch at the heel and toe represent Roman wheat, while the lace at the back of the leg bring to my mind the Colosseum.

The socks are worked top down. Instructions are given for DPNS, but the pattern is easily adjustable for Magic Loop or two circulars. The lace columns may be worked the same on both socks or knit as mirror images of one another. As written, the right sock incorporates a right-leaning decrease and the left, a left-leaning decrease.

When working charts in the round, read each row from right to left as a RS row.

Cuffs for sizes Size 7 and 9 are worked in K2, P2 ribbing, while cuffs for sizes 8 and 10 are worked in P2, K2 Ribbing. This is important so that the ribbing lines up properly with the Roman Wheat and Roman Columns lace patterns on the instep and back leg.

If a longer cuff is desired, one extra repeat of Roman Wheat Instep panel and two extra repeats of Roman Columns Back Leg Panel (Right or Left) should be worked. If this option is desired for size 8, two skeins of suggested yarn will be needed. For all other sizes, number of hanks suggested remains the same.

Roman Wheat Instep Panel (worked in the rnd over center 26 instep sts only)

Rnd 1: K4, K2tog, K3, YO, K1, YO, SSK, K5, K2tog, K3, YO, K1, YO, SSK, K1.
Rnd 2 and all even numbered rnds through 16: Knit.
Rnd 3: K3, K2tog, K4, YO, K1, YO, SSK, K4, K2tog, K4, YO, K1, YO, SSK, K1.
Rnd 5: K2, K2tog, K5, YO, K1, YO, SSK, K3, K2tog, K5, YO, K1, YO, SSK, K1.

Rnd 7: K1, K2tog, K6, YO, K1, YO, SSK, K2, K2tog, K6, YO, K1, YO, SSK, K1.
Rnd 9: K1, K2tog, YO, K1, YO, K3, SSK, K5, K2tog, YO, K1, YO, K3, SSK, K4.
Rnd 11: K1, K2tog, YO, K1, YO, K4, SSK, K4, K2tog, YO, K1, YO, K4, SSK, K3.
Rnd 13: K1, K2tog, YO, K1, YO, K5, SSK, K3, K2tog, YO, K1, YO, K5, SSK, K2.
Rnd 15: K1, K2tog, YO, K1, YO, K6, SSK, K2, K2tog, YO, K1, YO, K6, SSK, K1.
Rep Rnds 1-16 for pattern.

Roman Columns Back Leg Panel – Right (worked over center 26 sts on back leg only)

Rnd 1: (P2, K2tog, YO, K2, K2tog, YO) 3 times, P2.
Rnd 2: (P2, K6) 3 times, P2.
Rnd 3: (P2, K3, K2tog, YO, K1) 3 times, P2.
Rnds 4, 6, 8: Rep rnd 2.
Rnd 5: (P2, K2, K2tog, YO, K2) 3 times, P2.
Rnd 7: (P2, K1, K2tog, YO, K3) 3 times, P2.
Rep Rnds 1-8 for pattern.

Roman Columns Back Leg Panel – Left (worked over Center 26 sts on back leg only)

Rnd 1: (P2, YO, SSK, K2, YO, SSK) 3 times, P2.
Rnd 2: (P2, K6) 3 times, P2.
Rnd 3: (P2, K1, YO, SSK, K3) 3 times, P2.
Rnds 4, 6, 8: Rep Rnd 2.
Rnd 5: (P2, K2, YO, SSK, K2) 3 times, P2.
Rnd 7: (P2, K3, YO, SSK, K1) 3 times, P2.
Rep Rnds 1-8 for pattern.

K2, P2 Ribbing (worked in the rnd over multiples of 4 sts)
All Rnds: (K2, P2) to end.

P2, K2 Ribbing (worked in the rnd over multiples of 4 sts)
All Rnds: (P2, K2) to end.

DIRECTIONS

Loosely CO 52 (60, 68, 76) sts, dividing over DPNs as follows: 26 (30, 34, 38) sts on needle 1 and 13 (15, 17, 19) sts each on needles 2 and 3. Join to work in the rnd, being careful not to twist sts.

Cuff

Sizes 7 and 9 Only: Begin K2, P2 Ribbing.
Sizes 8 and 10 Only: Begin working P2, K2 Ribbing.
All Sizes: Work approximately 14 rnds or 1.5" of ribbing.

Leg

Needle 1: Work 0 (2, 4, 6) sts in designated ribbing as established, work Roman Wheat Instep Panel over 26 sts, work 0 (2, 4, 6) sts in ribbing as established. Needles 2 and 3: Work 0 (2, 4, 6) sts in rib as established, work Roman Columns Back Leg Chart (Right or Left) over 26 sts, work 0 (2, 4, 6) sts in ribbing as established.

Continue in this manner until Roman Wheat Instep Panel has been worked twice and chosen Back Leg Chart has been worked 4 times.

Heel

Heel is worked back and forth in rows over the established back leg sts, starting with a WS row. Sts are slipped as described. After slipping a st, the yarn will already be in position to work the next st.

Flap

Row 1 (WS): Sl 1 P-wise WYIB (K1, P1) to last st, K1.
Row 2 (RS): Sl 1 P-wise WYIF (P1, K1) to last st, P1.
Rep Rows 1 and 2 until 25 (29, 33, 37) total rows are completed, ending after a WS row.

Turn Heel

Row 1 (RS): Sl 1 P-wise WYIB, K14 (16, 18, 20) sts, SSK, K1, turn. 1 st dec.
Row 2 (WS): Sl 1 P-wise WYIF, P5, P2tog, P1, turn. 1 st dec.
Row 3: Sl 1, K to 1 st before gap, SSK over gap, K1, turn. 1 st dec.
Row 4: Sl 1, P to 1 st before gap, P2tog over gap, P1, turn. 1 st dec.
Rep Rows 3-4 until all Heel sts have been worked, ending with a WS row.

Gusset

K across all sts of heel and begin picking up heel flap sts as follows: PU 1 st at gap, then PU 13 (15, 17, 19) sts of flap and 1 st at gap. 15 (17, 19, 21) sts picked up.

Work 0 (2, 4, 6) sts in established ribbing on needle 1, work row 1 of Roman Wheat Instep Panel, work 0 (2, 4,6) sts in established ribbing. PU 1 st at gap, then 13 (15, 17, 19) sts of heel flap and 1 more st at last remaining gap. 15 (17, 19, 21) sts picked up.

K half the heel proper sts onto needle 2 (the same needle used to pick up the last sts worked). Then, changing needle, K second half of heel proper and K all picked up sts TBL.

Start of next rnd is here, and all sts should be on 3 needles once more. 26 (30, 34, 38) instep sts on needle 1 and heel/gusset sts divided evenly over needles 2 and 3. Note: it might be helpful to attach a removable stitch marker or safety pin at the start of the instep sts here to reinforce the beginning of rnd.

Needle 1: Work 0 (2, 4, 6) rib sts as established, work 26 sts of Roman Wheat Instep Panel as established, work 0 (2, 4, 6) rib sts as established. Needle 2: Work picked up sts TBL. Needle 3: Knit even.

Gusset Decreases

Rnd 1: Needle 1: Work 0 (2, 4, 6) sts in rib as set, work Roman Wheat Instep Panel as established, work 0 (2, 4, 6) sts in rib as established. Needle 2: K1, SSK, K to end of needle. Needle 3: K to last 3 sts of needle 3, K2tog, K1. 2 sts dec.
Rnd 2: Work instep sts as established, K to end of rnd.
Rep these two rnds until 52 (60, 68, 76) sts remain.

Foot

Work instep as established and K all other sts until Roman Wheat Instep Panel has been worked 6 times total.

Toe

Work ribbing as set, knitting all other sts, for 2 rnds. Then begin Seed Stitch toe as follows:
Rnd 1: (P1, K1) 2 (3, 4, 5) times, P1, K17, (P1, K1) 2 (3, 4, 5) times, K to end of rnd.
Rnd 2: (K1, P1) 3 (4, 5, 6) times, K15, (P1, K1) 2 (3, 4, 5) times end P1, K to end of rnd.
Rnd 3: (P1, K1 3 (4, 5, 6) times, P1, K13, (P1, K1) 3 (4, 5, 6) times, K to end of rnd.
Rnd 4: (K1, P1) 13 (15, 17, 19) times, K to end of rnd.
Rnd 5: (P1, K1) 13 (15, 17, 19) times, K to end of rnd.
Repeat Rnds 4 and 5 until approximately 0.75 (1, 1, 1.25)" less than desired foot length.

Decrease Rnd: Needle 1: SSK *K1 P1; rep from * to last 2 sts of needle, K2tog. Needle 2: K1, SSK, K to end of needle. Needle 3: K to last 3 sts, K2tog, K1. 4 sts dec.
Repeat Decrease Rnd 8 (10, 11, 13) more times. 16 (16, 20, 20) sts.

Finishing

Graft toe using Kitchener Stitch. Weave in ends, wash and block. Work second sock in the same manner, substituting the Roman Columns Back Leg Panel (Left) if desired.

Roman Wheat Instep Panel

26	25	24	23	22	21	20	19	18	17	16	15	14	13	12	11	10	9	8	7	6	5	4	3	2	1	
																										16
	\							O		O	/			\							O		O	/		15
																										14
		\						O		O	/				\						O		O	/		13
																										12
			\					O		O	/					\					O		O	/		11
																										10
				\				O		O	/						\				O		O	/		9
																										8
	\	O		O									/	\	O		O						/			7
																										6
	\	O		O						/				\	O		O				/					5
																										4
	\	O		O					/					\	O		O					/				3
																										2
	\	O		O				/						\	O		O						/			1

Legend

☐ **K** — Knit stitch

⊡ **P** — Purl stitch

◯ **yo** — Yarn Over

⟋ **k2tog** — Knit two stitches together as one stitch

⟍ **ssk** — Slip one stitch as if to knit. Slip another stitch as if to knit. Insert left-hand needle into front of these two stitches and knit them together.

Roman Columns Back Leg Panel - Right

26	25	24	23	22	21	20	19	18	17	16	15	14	13	12	11	10	9	8	7	6	5	4	3	2	1	
●	●							●	●							●	●							●	●	8
●	●				O	/		●	●				O	/		●	●			O	/			●	●	7
●	●							●	●							●	●							●	●	6
●	●			O	/			●	●			O	/			●	●			O	/			●	●	5
●	●							●	●							●	●							●	●	4
●	●		O	/				●	●		O	/				●	●		O	/				●	●	3
●	●							●	●							●	●							●	●	2
●	●	O	/			O	/	●	●	O	/			O	/	●	●	O	/			O	/	●	●	1

Roman Columns Back Leg Panel - Left

26	25	24	23	22	21	20	19	18	17	16	15	14	13	12	11	10	9	8	7	6	5	4	3	2	1	
●	●							●	●							●	●							●	●	8
●	●		\	O				●	●		\	O				●	●		\	O				●	●	7
●	●							●	●							●	●							●	●	6
●	●			\	O			●	●			\	O			●	●			\	O			●	●	5
●	●							●	●							●	●							●	●	4
●	●				\	O		●	●				\	O		●	●				\	O		●	●	3
●	●							●	●							●	●							●	●	2
●	●	\	O			\	O	●	●	\	O			\	O	●	●	\	O			\	O	●	●	1

ANNAGH SOCKS

by Luise O'Neill

FINISHED MEASUREMENTS

7.25 (7.75, 8.25)" finished foot circumference; 11" high.

YARN

Knit Picks Stroll Tonal Sock Yarn
(75% Superwash Merino Wool, 25% Nylon; 462 yards/100g): Malbec 27061, 1 skein.

NEEDLES

US 1.5 (2.5mm) DPNs or two 24" circular needles for two circulars technique, or one 32" or longer circular needle for Magic Loop technique, or size to obtain gauge.

NOTIONS

Yarn Needle
Stitch Markers
Cable Needle
Scrap Yarn or Stitch Holder

GAUGE

32 sts and 42 rows = 4" in St st in the rnd, blocked.
36 sts = 4" over Slip Stitch Pattern in the rnd, blocked.
36 sts = 3.75" over Cable Pattern in the rnd, blocked.

Notes:

The Crosses of Annagh is a traditional toe-tapping Irish reel – what better way to enjoy such a cheery tune than with a pair of multi-colored socks that pop just like the music.

These toe-up socks begin with a double-bar toe and are perfect for multi-colored yarns. The instep and front leg are worked in a slip stitch pattern flanked by cables on either side; the back leg is worked only in the cable pattern to provide a nice stretchy fabric. The short-row heel-flap heel means no picking up stitches!

All chart rows are RS rows and are read from right to left beginning at the bottom right.

Cable Pattern (worked in the rnd over 6 sts)
Rnd 1: K2, Sl2, K2.
Rnd 2: C1 over 2 right, C1 over 2 left.
Rnd 3: Sl1, K4, Sl1.
Rnd 4: K6.
Rep Rnds 1-4 for pattern.

Slip Stitch Pattern (worked in the rnd over 16 sts)
Rnd 1: *Sl1, K1; rep from * 7 times.
Rnd 2: *Sl1, P1; rep from * 7 times.
Rnds 3 and 4: K16.
Rnd 5: *K1, Sl1; rep from * 7 times.
Rnd 6: *P1, Sl1; rep from * 7 times.
Rnds 7 and 8: K16.
Rep Rnds 1-8 for pattern.

Judy's Magic Cast On: Tutorial on Knit Picks website can be found at http://tutorials.knitpicks.com/judys-magic-cast-on/.

Wrap and Turn (W&T): Tutorial on Knit Picks website can be found at http://tutorials.knitpicks.com/wptutorials/short-rows-wrap-and-turn-or-wt/.

Make 1 Left (M1L): Insert tip of LH needle, from back to front, to lift left leg of st 2 rows below first st on RH needle; K lifted loop TBL.

Make 1 Right (M1R): Insert tip of RH needle, from back to front, to lift right leg of st 1 row below first st on LH needle and place lifted loop onto LH needle, K lifted loop.

DIRECTIONS

Directions are written for the smallest size; changes for larger sizes are given in parentheses. When only one number is given, it applies to all sizes.

Using Judy's Magic Cast On, CO 20 sts (10 sts on each needle). Place an end of rnd marker. Note: This cast on includes one knit rnd. If you chose an alternate cast on that does not include this, knit one rnd before working the following directions.

An additional marker is placed in the next rnd to mark the division between the sole and instep sts.

Toe

Toe Rnd 1 (Inc Rnd): *K1, M1R, K8, M1L, K1*, PM; rep from * to *. 24 sts.

Toe Rnds 2, 4, 6, 8, 10: Knit.

Toe Rnd 3 (Inc Rnd): *K2, M1R, K8, M1L, K2, SM; rep from *. 28 sts.

Toe Rnd 5 (Inc Rnd): *K3, M1R, K8, M1L, K3, SM; rep from *. 32 sts.

Toe Rnd 7 (Inc Rnd): *K4, M1R, K8, M1L, K4, SM; rep from *. 36 sts.

Toe Rnd 9 (Inc Rnd): *K5, M1R, K8, M1L, K5, SM; rep from *. 40 sts.

Toe Rnd 11 (Inc Rnd): *K4, M1L, K to 4 sts before M, M1R, K4, SM; rep from *. 44 sts.

Rep previous 2 rnds 4 (5, 6) more times. 60 (64, 68) sts.

Next Rnd (Inc Rnd): K to M, SM, K4, M1L, K to 4 sts before M, M1R, K4. 30 (32, 34) sole sts, 32 (34, 36) instep sts. 2 sts inc.

Foot

Rnd 1: K to M, SM, K1 (2, 3), work Cable Pattern over next 6 sts, P1, work Slip Stitch Pattern over next 16 sts, P1, work Cable Pattern over next 6 sts, K1 (2, 3).

Rnd 2: K to M, SM, P1 (2, 3), work Cable Pattern over next 6 sts, P1, work Slip Stitch Pattern over next 16 sts, P1, work Cable Pattern over next 6 sts, P1 (2, 3).

Rep these two rnds until work measures 5 (6, 6.25)" or 3.25 (3.5, 3.75)" shorter than desired foot length ending having completed a Rnd 1 of foot pattern.

Next Rnd (Inc Rnd): K6 (7, 7), M1L, PM, K18 (18, 20), PM, M1R, K6 (7, 7), SM, continue in pattern over instep sts. 2 sts inc.

Gusset

Gusset Rnd 1: (K to M, SM) 3 times, continue in pattern over instep sts.

Gusset Rnd 2 (Inc Rnd): K to M, M1L, SM, K to M, SM, M1R, K to M, SM, continue in pattern over instep sts. 2 sts inc.

Rep these two rnds until there are 48 (50, 54) sole sts, ending having completed an Inc Rnd.

Heel

Turning the Heel

The instep sts will not be worked in this section; the 15 (16, 17) sts on either end of the sole section also will be set aside until after the heel is turned. The center 18 (18, 20) sts of the sole form the base of the heel cap.

Heel Row 1 (RS-Inc Row): K15 (16, 17), remove M; place 15 (16, 17) sts just worked onto a stitch holder or scrap yarn; K1, KFB, K14 (14, 16), Sl2 to RH needle and remove M, place next 15 (16, 17) sts on stitch holder or scrap yarn, Sl2 back to LH needle, W&T. 19 (19, 21) sts on sole needle. Only these sts will be worked over the following rows.

Heel Row 2 (WS-Inc Row): Sl1 WYIF, PFB, P to last 2 sts, W&T. 1 st inc.

Heel Row 3 (Inc Row): Sl1, KFB, K to last 3 sts, W&T. 1 st inc.

Heel Row 4 (Inc Row): Sl1 WYIF, PFB, P to last 3 sts, W&T. 1 st inc.

Rep Heel Rows 3-4 leaving one more st unworked for each set of rows e.g. on Heel Rows 5 and 6 four sts are left unworked; on Heel Rows 7 and 8 five sts are left unworked, and so on until there are 30 (32, 34) sts on the needle.

The decreases worked at the end of the next two rows form a small gap; this is the gap referred to in the following Heel Flap section. The decreases use one st from either side of that gap.

Next Row (RS): Knitting any wraps along with their corresponding sts, Sl1, K to last st, Sl1 to RH needle, transfer 15 (16, 17) held sts onto LH needle, Sl1 back to LH needle, SSK. Turn. 1 st dec.

Next Row (WS): Purling any wraps along with their corresponding sts, Sl1 WYIF, P to last st, Sl1 WYIF to RH needle, transfer 15 (16, 17) held sts onto LH needle, Sl1 WYIF back to LH needle, P2TOG. Turn. 1 st dec.

Heel Flap

Heel Flap Row 1 (RS): Sl1, * K1, Sl1; rep from * to 1 st before gap, SSK. Turn. 1 st dec.

Heel Flap Row 2 (WS): Sl1 WYIF, P to 1 st before gap, P2tog. Turn. 1 st dec.

Rep these two rows until all previously held sts have been incorporated into the heel flap sts. 30 (32, 34) heel flap sts.

Leg

Knitting in the rnd resumes.

Next Rnd (Inc Rnd-move end of rnd M): K3 (4, 5), M1 *K5, M1; rep from * 4 times, K2 (3, 4), remove M, continue in pattern on front leg sts, remove end of rnd M, K1 (2, 3), replace end of rnd M. 36 (38, 40) back leg sts, 32 (34, 36) front leg sts.

In the following rnd, match the Cable Pattern on the back and front leg sts.

Next Rnd: *Work Cable Pattern over next 6 sts, P1; rep from * 3 times, work Cable Pattern over next 6 sts, P2 (4, 6), work Cable Pattern over next 6 sts, P1, work Slip Stitch Pattern over next 16 sts, P1, work Cable Pattern over next 6 sts, P2 (4, 6).

Next Rnd: *Work Cable Pattern over next 6 sts, P1; rep from * 3 times, work Cable Pattern over next 6 sts, K2 (4, 6), work Cable Pattern over next 6 sts, P1, work Slip Stitch Pattern over next 16 sts, P1, work Cable Pattern over next 6 sts, K2 (4, 6).

Rep these two rnds until sock from bottom of heel measures 10".

Cuff

Ribbing Rnd, Size 7.25" Only: (K2, P2, K2, P1) 4 times, (K2, P2) 10 times.

Ribbing Rnd, Size 7.75" Only: (K2, P2, K2, P1) 5 times, K2, P1, (K2, P2) 7 times, (K2, P1) twice.

Ribbing Rnd, Size 8.25" Only: (K2, P2, K2, P1) 4 times, (K2, P2) 12 times.

All Sizes: Rep Ribbing Rnd nine times.

BO using a stretchy bind off. Cut yarn leaving a 6" tail.

Finishing

Weave in ends, wash and block.

Legend

☐ **K**
Knit stitch

⊡ **P**
Purl stitch

Ⅴ **slip**
Slip stitch as if to purl, with yarn in back.

☐ **Pattern Repeat**

◪ **c1 over 2 right**
sl2 to CN, hold in back. k1, k2 from CN.

◪ **c1 over 2 left**
sl1 to CN, hold in front. k2, k1 from CN.

Cable Pattern

6	5	4	3	2	1	
						4
Ⅴ					Ⅴ	3
						2
			Ⅴ	Ⅴ		1

Slip Stitch Pattern

2	1	
		8
		7
Ⅴ	●	6
Ⅴ		5
		4
		3
●	Ⅴ	2
	Ⅴ	1

BAKEWELL

by M K Nance

FINISHED MEASUREMENTS

6.75 (7.75, 8.75, 9.75)" foot
circumference; foot length is adjustable

YARN

Knit Picks Hawthorne Kettle Dye
(80% Superwash Fine Highland
Wool, 20% Polyamide (Nylon); 357
yards/100g): MC Wisp 26692, 1 skein.
Knit Picks Hawthorne Multi
(80% Superwash Fine Highland Wool,
20% Polyamide (Nylon;) 357 yards/100g):
C1 Springwater 27422, 1 skein.

NEEDLES

US 0 (2mm) DPNs or two 24" circular
needles for two circulars technique, or one
32" or longer circular needle for Magic
Loop technique, or size to obtain gauge.

NOTIONS

Yarn Needle
Stitch Markers
Cable Needle

GAUGE

36 sts and 50 rnds = 4" in St st in the
rnd, blocked.

For pattern support, contact
mknanceknit@gmail.com

Notes:

This is a basic toe up gusset sock which uses two different colors. There is enough interest for well-seasoned knitters, but it is also easy enough for an adventurous beginner. The pattern mimics the top of a Bakewell tart. Only one color is carried per round, so the pattern looks more complex than it really is. Slipped stitches are slipped purlwise with yarn held to the wrong side. It may be easier to do the cables without a cable needle as they are all one st over one st.

When working charts in the rnd, read each row from right to left as a RS row.

Turkish CO Method

Make a slip knot and place it on one needle. Place 2 needles parallel, one on top of the other, with pointed ends facing the same direction and with slip knot loop on bottom needle. Take yarn and wrap around back, over the top and back to the front, looping around both needles. Make each loop to the right of the last loop. Repeat until there are enough loops for half your needed CO sts, minus 1. Wrap yarn around the top needle once more and bring the yarn between the needles. With another needle, knit the sts on the top needle, then knit the sts on the bottom needle. If using circulars, you can pull the bottom needle through the loops so the loops are now on the cable and use it to knit the loops on the top needle.

1/1 Right Cross (1/1 RC): Sl1 to CN, hold in back, K1, K1 from CN.
1/1 Left Cross (1/1 LC): Sl1 to CN, hold in front, K1, K1 from CN.
To work cables without a CN, see tutorial here: http://tutorials.knitpicks.com/learn-to-cable-without-a-cable-needle/.

K2, P2 Rib (worked in the rnd over multiple of 4 sts)
All Rnds: *K2, P2; rep from * to end.

Wrap and Turn (W&T)

Work until the st to be wrapped. If knitting: Bring the yarn to the front of the work, Sl next st as if to purl, return the yarn to the back; turn work and slip wrapped st onto the RH needle. Continue across the row. If purling: Bring yarn to the back of work, Sl next st as if to purl, return the yarn to the front; turn work and slip wrapped st onto RH needle. Continue across the row.

Picking up Wraps

Work to the wrapped st. If knitting, insert the RH needle under the wrap, then through the wrapped st K-wise. Knit the st and the wrap together. If purling, slip the wrapped st P-wise onto the RH needle, and use the LH needle to lift the wrap and place them on the RH needle. Sl the wrap and st back on the LH needle and purl tog.

Bakewell Right (worked in the rnd over 21 sts)
Rnd 1: In MC K6, (1/1 RC, K3) x 3.
Rnd 2: In C1 P6, (Sl 1, P4) x 3.
Rnd 3: In MC K5, (1/1 RC, K3) x 2, 1/1 RC, K4.
Rnd 4: In C1 P5, (Sl 1, P4) x 2, Sl 1, P5.
Rnd 5: In MC K4, (1/1 RC, K3) x 2, 1/1 RC, K5.
Rnd 6: In C1 (P4, Sl 1) x 3, P6.
Rnd 7: In MC K4, (1/1 LC, K3) x 2, 1/1 LC, K5.

Rnd 8: In C1 rep Rnd 4.
Rnd 9: In MC K5, (1/1 LC, K3) x 2, 1/1 LC, K4.
Rnd 10: In C1 rep Rnd 2.
Rnd 11: In MC K6, (1/1 LC, K3) x 3.
Rnd 12: In C1 P7, (Sl 1, P4) x 2, Sl 1, P3.
Rep Rnds 1-12 for pattern.

Bakewell Left (in the rnd over 21 sts)
Rnd 1: In MC (K3, 1/1 LC) x 3, K6.
Rnd 2: In C1 (P4, Sl 1) x 3, p6.
Rnd 3: In MC K4, (1/1 LC, K3) x 2, 1/1 LC, K5.
Rnd 4: In C1 P5, (Sl 1, P4) x 2, Sl 1, P5.
Rnd 5: In MC K5, (1/1 LC, K3) x 2, 1/1 LC, K4.
Rnd 6: In C1 P6, (Sl 1, P4) x 3.
Rnd 7: In MC K5, (1/1 RC, K3) x 2, 1/1 RC, K4.
Rnd 8: In C1 rep Rnd 4.
Rnd 9: In MC K4, (1/1 RC, K3) x 2, 1/1 RC, K5.
Rnd 10: In C1 rep Rnd 2.
Rnd 11: In MC (K3, 1/1 RC) x 3, K6.
Rnd 12: In C1 P3, (Sl 1, P4) x 2, Sl 1, P7.
Rep Rnds 1-12 for pattern.

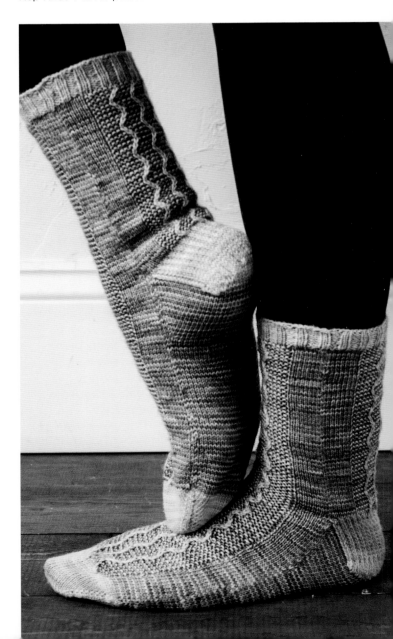

DIRECTIONS

Right Sock

Toe

With MC using the Turkish method, CO 26 (30, 34, 38) sts. 13 (15, 17, 19) sts. PM and join to work in the rnd.

Inc Rnd: *K1, M1, K11 (13, 15, 17), M1, K1; PM, rep from * once more. 30 (34, 38, 42) sts total, 15 (17, 19, 21) sts each for the instep and sole.

Next Rnd: Knit.

Inc Rnd: *K1, M1, K to 1 st before M, M1, K1, SM; rep from * once more. 4 sts inc.

Rep last 2 rounds 6 (7, 8, 9) more times, 58 (66, 74, 82) total sts, 29 (33, 37, 41) sts each for instep and sole.

Foot

Next Rnd: In MC K4 (6, 8, 10), PM, K21 in Bakewell Right, PM, K4 (6, 8, 10), SM, K29 (33, 37, 41).

Next Rnd: In C1 K4 (6, 8, 10), PM, K21 in Bakewell Right, PM, K4 (6, 8, 10), SM, K29 (33, 37, 41).

Work in pattern as established until piece measures 2.5" less than desired foot length ending with a C1 rnd.

Gusset

Inc Rnd: In MC work instep sts in pattern, SM, K1, M1, K to last st, M1, K1. 2 sts inc.

Next Rnd: In C1 work instep sts in pattern, SM, K to the end.

Rep last 2 rnds 9 (10, 11, 12) more times. 78 (88, 98, 108) total sts, 29 (33, 37, 41) instep sts, and 49 (55, 61, 67) sole sts.

Turn Heel

Next Rnd: Work instep sts in pattern, SM. Heel turn is now worked back and forth in rows over sole sts.

Shape heel, using short-rows as follows:

Short Row 1 (RS): K33 (37, 41, 44), KFB, K1, W&T. 1 st inc.

Short Row 2 (WS): P20 (22, 24, 26), PFB, P1, W&T. 1 st inc.

Short Row 3: K to 5 sts before previously wrapped st, KFB, K1, W&T. 1 st inc.

Short Row 4: P to 5 sts before previously wrapped st, PFB, K1, W&T. 1 st inc.

Rep Short Rows 3 and 4 twice more. 57 (63, 69, 75) sole sts, with 4 wrapped sts at each side.

Next Rnd: With RS facing, in MC K to end of sole sts, PU wrapped sts, break MC then work instep sts in pattern in C1, break C1.

Heel Flap

Row 1 (RS): In MC K42 (47, 52, 55), PU wrapped sts, SSK, turn. 1 st dec.

Row 2 (WS): Sl 1, P27 (31, 35, 39), P2tog, turn. 1 st dec.

Row 3: (Sl 1, K1) 14 (16, 18, 20) times, SSK, turn. 1 st dec.

Rep Rows 2-3 12 (13, 14, 15) more times, then work Row 2 once more. 29 (33, 37, 41) heel sts remain. 58 (66, 74, 82) total sts.

Leg

Next Rnd: In MC K4 (6, 8, 10), PM, work 21 sts in Bakewell Right, PM, K4 (6, 8, 10), SM, K4 (6, 8, 10), PM, work 21 sts in Bakewell Right, PM, K4 (6, 8, 10).

Next Rnd: In C1 K4 (6, 8, 10), PM, work 21 sts in Bakewell Right, PM, K4 (6, 8, 10), SM, K4 (6, 8, 10), PM, work 21 sts in Bakewell Right, PM, K4 (6, 8, 10).

Rep last 2 rnds as established until leg measures 5", or 1.5" less than desired length ending with a C1 rnd. Break C1.

Cuff

Next Rnd: In MC, K2tog, K27 (31, 35, 39), K2tog, K27 (31, 35, 39). 56 (64, 72, 80) sts.

Work in K2, P2 Rib for 1.5", or until sock measures desired length. BO loosely.

Left Sock

Work as Right sock except using Bakewell Left.

Finishing

Weave in ends, wash and block.

Bakewell Left

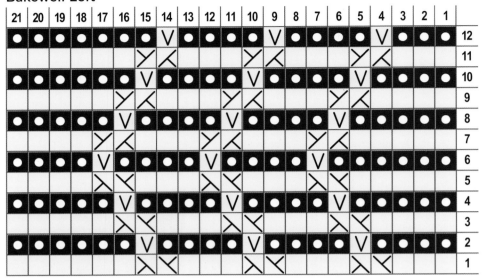

Bakewell Right

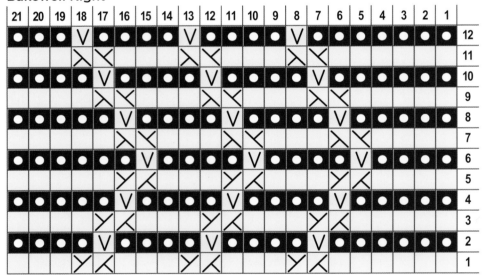

Legend

K Knit stitch	**MC**	**slip** Slip stitch as if to purl, with yarn in back.
P Purl stitch	**CC**	**Left Twist** sl1 to CN, hold in front. k1, k1 from CN.
		Right Twist Skip the first st, knit into 2nd st, then knit skipped st. Slip both sts off LH needle.

CATHEDRAL ARCHES

by Megan Dial

FINISHED MEASUREMENTS

8.5" circumference x 8.5 (9.5, 10.5)" long
from back of heel to tip of toe; to fit US
women's shoe sizes 5-6.5 (7-9, 10-11)

YARN

Knit Picks Gloss Fingering
(70% Merino Wool, 30% Silk; 220
yards/50g): Sterling 27019, 1 skein.

NEEDLES

US 1 (2.25mm) DPNs, or size to
obtain gauge.

NOTIONS

Yarn Needle
Stitch Markers
Cable Needle

GAUGE

35 sts and 44 rows = 4" over Charted
Pattern in the rnd, blocked.

Notes:

Inspired by the soaring arched windows of the great gothic churches, Cathedral Arches Socks feature candle-flame cables, seed stitch, and mini-twists -- interesting to knit while showing the gorgeous solid or tonal colors of the chosen yarn to greatest effect. Heel flap and gusset construction allows the elegant large cable to continue all the way through the heel.

When working charts in the round, read each row from right to left as a RS row. To work flat, read RS rows (odd numbers) from right to left, and WS rows (even numbers) from left to right.

Seed Stitch Pattern (in the rnd over an even number of sts)
Rnd 1: *K1, P1: rep from *
Rnd 2: K the P sts and P the K sts.
Rep Rnd 2 for pattern.

For a video demonstration of how to work Kitchener St, see http://tutorials.knitpicks.com/wptutorials/kitchener-stitch/.

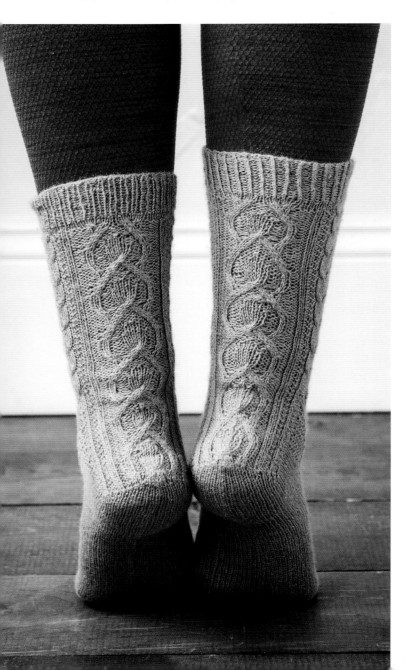

DIRECTIONS

Cuff

CO 74 sts. Arrange on 4 DPNs with 18, 19, 18, 19 sts on Needles 1-4 respectively, PM, and join in the rnd, being careful not to twist sts.
Rib Rnd: *K1 Tbl, P1; rep from * to end.
Rep Rib Rnd for 15 more rnds.

Leg

K 3 rnds.
Work Leg Chart Rows 1-16 4 times, rep chart row twice across rnd, ending with Row 16. Piece measures approximately 6" from CO edge.

Heel

Place first 37 sts of rnd onto one needle. Heel will be worked back and forth in rows on these 37 sts; remaining sts will be worked later for instep. Work Rows 1-16 of Heel Flap Chart twice.

Turn Heel
Work short rows as follows:
Row 1 (RS): K20, Ssk, K1, turn. 1 st dec.
Row 2 (WS): Sl 1, P4, P2tog, P1, turn. 1 st dec.
Row 3: Sl 1, K to 1 st before break created by turn on previous row, Ssk, K1, turn. 1 st dec.
Row 4: Sl 1, P to 1 st before break created by turn on previous row, P2tog, P1, turn. 1 st dec.
Work Rows 3 and 4 six more times, 21 sts remain on heel.

Shape Gusset
Gusset Set-up Rnd: K21 sts, PU and K 16 sts along edge of heel flap: work Row 1 of Leg chart, PU and K 16 sts along other edge of heel flap, K11 (from Needle 1).
Sts should be arranged on DPNs as follows: Needle 1 = 26 sts, Needle 2 = 19 sts, Needle 3 = 18 sts, Needle 4 = 27 sts. 90 sts total.
Gusset Rnd 1: Needle 1: K16, work in Seed st to last 2 sts, K2; Needles 2 and 3: Work next row of Leg Chart; Needle 4: K2, work Seed st to last 17 sts, K17.
Repeat Gusset Rnd 1 twice more.
Gusset Rnd 2: Needle 1: K16, work Seed st to last 3 sts, K2tog, K1; Needles 2 and 3: Next row of Leg Chart; Needle 4: K1, Ssk, work Seed st to last 17 sts, K17. 2 sts dec.
Work *Gusset Rnd 1 twice and then Gusset Rnd 2 once; rep from * 7 times more, until 74 sts remain.

Foot

Work evenly as established until foot measures approximately 7.25 (8.25, 9.25)" from back of heel ending with a Row 16 or 10 of Leg Chart.
Toe Set-up Rnd: K18, Ssk, K35, Ssk, K17. 72 sts.
Dec Rnd: Needles 1 and 3: K to last 3 sts, K2tog, K1; Needles 2 and 4: K1, Ssk, K to end of needle. 4 sts dec.
Knit evenly, repeating Dec Rnd every 4th rnd once, every 3rd rnd twice, every 2nd rnd 3 times, then every rnd 3 times. 36 sts.

Final Dec Rnd: K7, K2tog, Ssk, K14, K2tog, Ssk, K7. 32 sts.

Finishing

Sl all sts from Needle 4 to Needle 1 and from Needle 3 to Needle 2. Break yarn leaving a tail of approximately 24" for finishing. Thread tail through yarn needle and use the Kitchener Stitch technique to graft remaining sts together neatly.

Weave in ends, wash and block.

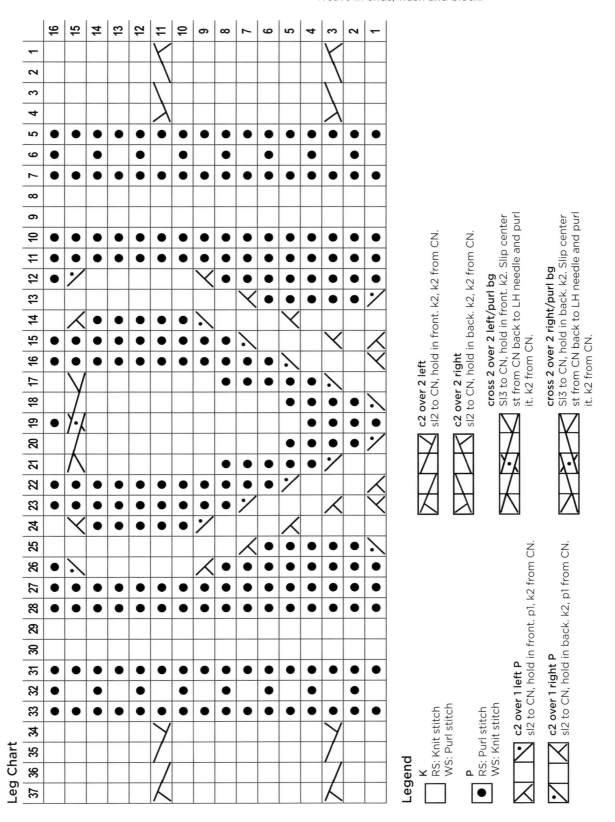

Legend

K
RS: Knit stitch
WS: Purl stitch

P
RS: Purl stitch
WS: Knit stitch

c2 over 1 left P
sl2 to CN, hold in front. p1, k2 from CN.

c2 over 1 right P
sl2 to CN, hold in back. k2, p1 from CN.

c2 over 2 left
sl2 to CN, hold in front. k2, k2 from CN.

c2 over 2 right
sl2 to CN, hold in back. k2, k2 from CN.

cross 2 over 2 left/purl bg
Sl3 to CN, hold in front. k2. Slip center st from CN back to LH needle and purl it. k2 from CN.

cross 2 over 2 right/purl bg
Sl3 to CN, hold in back. k2. Slip center st from CN back to LH needle and purl it. k2 from CN.

Heel Flap Chart

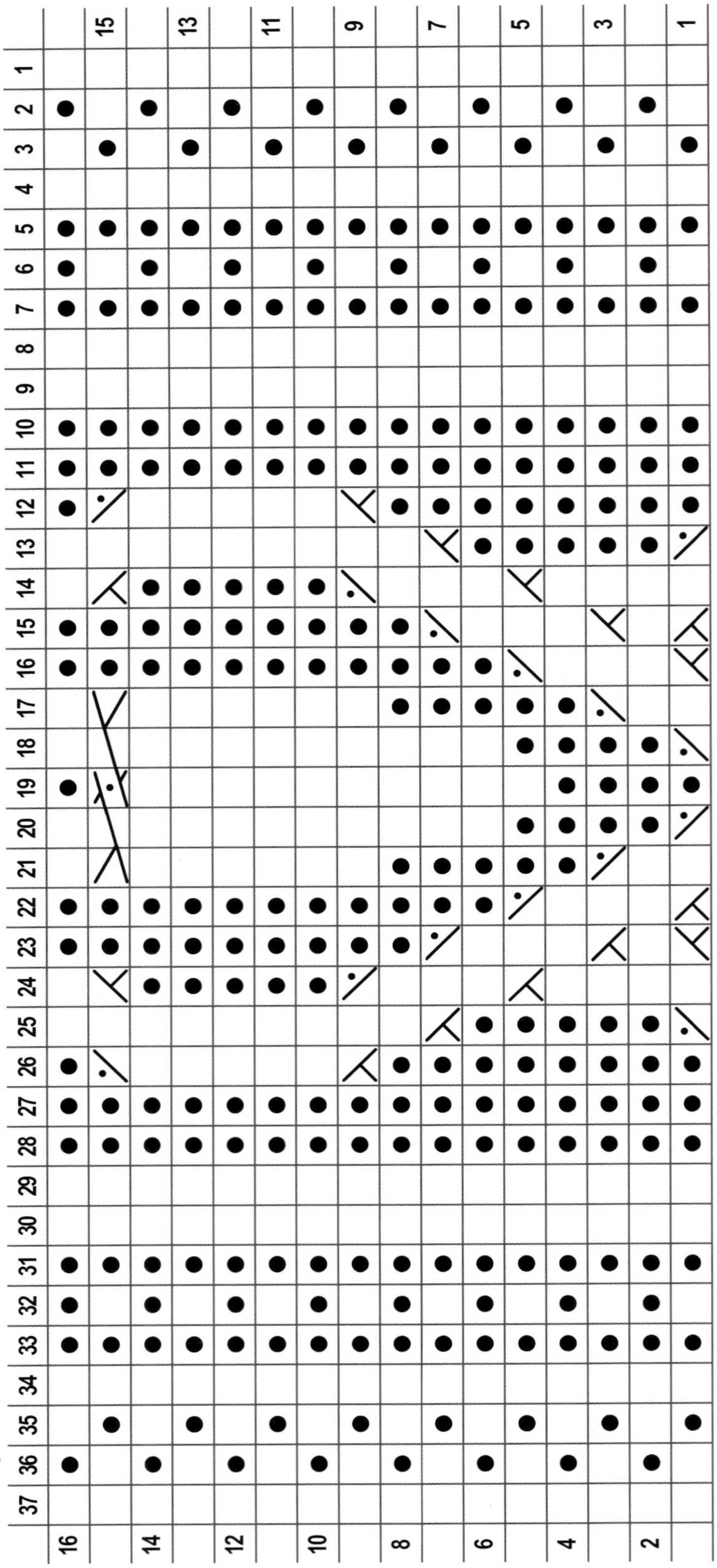

CORRANDULLA SOCKS

by Luise O'Neill

FINISHED MEASUREMENTS
7.5 (8, 8.5)" finished foot circumference;
11" high.

YARN
Knit Picks Stroll Sock Yarn
(75% Superwash Merino Wool, 25%
Nylon; 231 yards/50g): Forest Heather
24589, 2 balls.

NEEDLES
US 1.5 (2.5mm) DPNs or two 24" circular
needles for two circulars technique, or one
32" or longer circular needle for Magic
Loop technique, or size to obtain gauge.

NOTIONS
Yarn Needle
Stitch Markers
Cable Needle
Scrap Yarn or Stitch Holder

GAUGE
32 sts and 42 rows = 4" in St st in the
rnd, blocked.
32 sts = 3.5" over Chart A pattern in the
rnd, blocked.

The Road to Corrandulla is a sprightly reel evoking visions of the beautiful, lusciously green Irish countryside in county Galway and inviting your toes to dance. Embrace your inner sprite and let this traditional tune transport you to a place of joy and merriment!

The Corrandulla Socks are knit toe-up and begin with a wide toe. The instep is worked in a single-cable lattice that grows from a double-V cable. Each lattice diamond holds a pert little leaf that springs from a cable base. This lattice-leaf pattern expands to fill the instep and continues both on the front and back leg. The double-bar gusset leads into a short-row, heel-flap heel which means no picking up stitches. The heel flap is worked in an Eye of Partridge pattern that beautifully echoes the main pattern lattice motif. Part way up the leg, the lattice-leaf pattern morphs into single, offset diagonal cables allowing flexibility for adjusting the leg length for these socks; these cable tendrils sprout tiny buds for a lovely final flourish.

This pattern is charted only. All chart rows are RS rows and are read from right to left beginning at the bottom right. Chart A is split over 2 pages. The cable stitches shown with a yellow background are 'flex' cables that are worked as a right cross on one sock and left cross on the second sock to create a mirrored effect.

Make 1 Left (M1L): Insert tip of LH needle, from back to front, to lift left leg of st 2 rows below first st on RH needle; K lifted loop TBL.

Make 1 Right (M1R): Insert tip of RH needle, from back to front, to lift right leg of st 1 row below first st on LH needle and place lifted loop onto LH needle, K lifted loop.

Judy's Magic Cast On: Tutorial on Knit Picks website can be found at http://tutorials.knitpicks.com/judys-magic-cast-on/.

Wrap and Turn (W&T): Tutorial on Knit Picks website can be found at http://tutorials.knitpicks.com/wptutorials/short-rows-wrap-and-turn-or-wt/.

DIRECTIONS

Toe

Using Judy's Magic Cast On, CO 20 sts (10 sts on each needle). Place an end of rnd marker. Note: This CO includes one knit rnd. If your chosen CO does not include this, knit one rnd before working the following directions.

An additional M is placed in the next rnd to mark the division between the sole and instep sts.
Rnd 1 (Inc Rnd): KFB, K7, KFB, K1, PM, KFB, K7, KFB, K1. 24 sts.
Rnd 2 (Inc Rnd): *KFB, K to 2 sts before M, KFB, K1, SM; rep from *. 28 sts.
Rep this rnd twice. 32, then 36 sts.
Rnd 5: Knit.
Rnd 6 (Inc Rnd): Rep Rnd 2. 40 sts.
Rep previous 2 rnds until there are 60 (64, 68) sts on the needle(s).
Next Rnd (Inc Rnd): K to M, SM, KFB, K to 2 sts before M, KFB, K1. 30 (32, 34) sole sts, 32 (34, 36) instep sts.
Rep this rnd once. 30 (32, 34) sole sts, 34 (36, 38) instep sts.

Foot

When working Chart A, work Rows 1-70 then Rows 43-70 once more. The second completion of Row 70 occurs part way up the leg.
Foot Rnd 1: K to M, SM, K1 (2, 3), work Chart A over next 32 sts, K1 (2, 3).
Foot Rnd 2: K to M, SM, P1 (2, 3), work Chart A over next 32 sts, P1 (2, 3).
Rep these two rnds working subsequent rows of chart until sock measures 5 (6, 6.25)" or 3.25 (3.25, 3.75)" shorter than desired foot length, ending having completed an odd-numbered chart row.

Gusset

Two additional M are placed in the next rnd to mark the gusset inc points.
First Setup Rnd (Inc Rnd): K14 (15, 16), PM, M1L, K2, M1R, PM, K to M, SM; continue in pattern over instep sts. 32 (34, 36) sole sts.
Gusset Rnd 1: (K to M, SM) 3 times; continue in pattern over instep sts.
Gusset Rnd 2 (Inc Rnd): K to M, SM, M1L, K to M, M1R, SM, K to M, SM; continue in pattern over instep sts. 34 (36, 38) sole sts.
Rep previous two rnds 3 times. 40 (42, 44) sole sts.
Next Rnd: Rep Gusset Rnd 1 removing the two gusset M. These are repositioned in the next rnd.
Second Setup Rnd (Inc Rnd): K19 (20, 21), PM, M1L, K2, M1R, PM, K to M, SM; continue in pattern over instep sts. 42 (44, 46) sole sts.
Next Rnd: (K to M, SM) 3 times; continue in pattern over instep sts.
Next Rnd (Inc Rnd): K to M, SM, M1L, K to M, M1R, SM, K to M, SM; continue in pattern over instep sts. 44 (46, 48) sole sts.
Rep previous two rnds until there are 52 (54, 58) sole sts.
Next Rnd: Rep Gusset Rnd 1 removing the two gusset M.

Heel

Turning the Heel

The instep sts are not worked in this section and the 17 (18, 19) sts at either end of the sole section are also set aside until after the heel is turned; the center 18 (18, 20) sts form the base of the heel cap.

Heel Row 1 (RS-Inc Row): K17 (18, 19), transfer these sts to a st holder or scrap yarn, K1, KFB, K14 (14, 16), Sl2 to RH needle, transfer next 17 (18, 19) sts to a st holder or scrap yarn, Sl2 back to LH needle, W&T. 19 (19, 21) heel sts on the needle. Only these sts will be worked over the following rows.

Heel Row 2 (WS-Inc Row): Sl1 WYIF, PFB, P to last 2 sts, W&T. 1 st inc.

Heel Row 3 (Inc Row): Sl1, KFB, K to last 3 sts, W&T. 1 st inc.

Heel Row 4 (Inc Row): Sl1 WYIF, PFB, P to last 3 sts, W&T. 1 st inc.

Rep previous two rnds leaving one more st unworked for each set of rows e.g. on Heel Row 5 and 6 leave 4 sts unworked, on Heel Row 7 and 8 leave 5 sts unworked, until there are 30 (32, 34) heel sts on the needle.

The dec worked at the end of the next two rows form a small gap; this is the gap referred to in the following Heel Flap section. The decreases use one st from either side of that gap.

Next Row (RS): Knitting any wraps along with their corresponding sts, Sl1, K to last st, Sl1 to RH needle, transfer 17 (18, 19) held sts to LH needle, Sl1 back to LH needle, SSK. Turn. 1 st dec.

Next Row (WS): Purling any wraps along with their corresponding sts, Sl1 WYIF, P to last st, Sl1 WYIF to RH needle, transfer 17 (18, 19) held sts to LH needle, Sl1 WYIF back to LH needle, P2tog. Turn. 1 st dec.

Heel Flap

Heel Flap Row 1 (RS): Sl1, *K1, Sl1; rep from * to 1 st before gap, SSK. Turn. 1 st dec.

Heel Flap Row 2 (WS): Sl1 WYIF, P to 1 st before gap, P2tog. Turn. 1 st dec.

Heel Flap Row 3: Sl1, K1, *K1, Sl1; rep from * to 2 sts before gap, K1, SSK. Turn. 1 st dec.

Heel Flap Row 4: Sl1 WYIF, P to 1 st before gap, P2tog. Turn. 1 st dec.

Rep these four rows until all previously held sts have been incorporated into the heel flap sts. 30 (32, 34) heel flap sts, 64 (68, 72) total sts.

Leg

Knitting in the rnd resumes.

Setup Rnd (Inc Rnd-end of rnd M moved): K6 (7, 8), M1, (K6, M1) 3 times, K6 (7, 8), remove M, continue in pattern over instep sts. Remove end of rnd M, P1 (2, 3), replace M. 68 (72, 76) sts.

Leg Rnd 1: *Work Chart A over next 32 sts, K2 (4, 6); rep from *.

Leg Rnd 2: *Work Chart A over next 32 sts, P2 (4, 6); rep from *.

Rep these two rnds until Row 70 of Chart A is completed a second time.

Next Rnd: *Work Chart B over next 32 sts, K2 (4, 6); rep from *.

Next Rnd: *Work Chart B over next 32 sts, P2 (4, 6); rep from *.

Rep these two rnds working Rows 1-14 of Chart B, then rep Rows 7-14 until leg, from bottom of heel, measures 8.75" or 2.25" shorter than desired height ending having completed a Row 14 of chart; then working Rows 15-25 of chart.

Cuff

Ribbing Rnd Size 7.5" Only: *(K1, P1, K2, P1) 3 times, K2, (P1, K2, P1, K1) 3 times, P2; rep from *.

Ribbing Rnd Size 8" Only: *(K1, P1, K2, P1) 3 times, K2, (P1, K2, P1, K1) 3 times, P1, K2, P1; rep from *.

Ribbing Rnd Size 8.5" Only : *(K1, P1, K2, P1) 3 times, K2, (P1, K2, P1, K1) 3 times, P2, K2, P2; rep from *.

All Sizes: Rep Ribbing Rnd nine times.

Bind off using a stretchy bind off.

Finishing

Weave in ends, wash and block.

Chart A

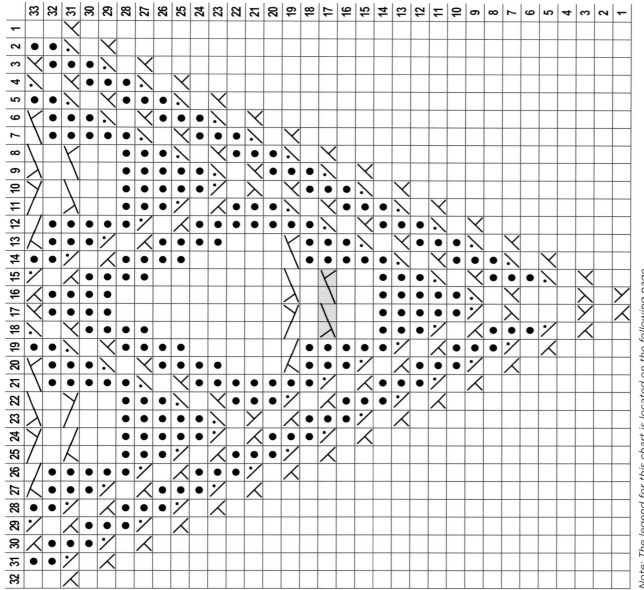

Note: The legend for this chart is located on the following page.

Chart B

Legend

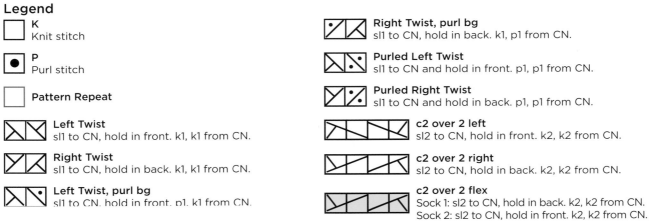

	K
☐	Knit stitch

	P
☐•	Purl stitch

	Pattern Repeat
☐	

Left Twist
sl1 to CN, hold in front. k1, k1 from CN.

Right Twist
sl1 to CN, hold in back. k1, k1 from CN.

Left Twist, purl bg
sl1 to CN, hold in front. p1, k1 from CN.

Right Twist, purl bg
sl1 to CN, hold in back. k1, p1 from CN.

Purled Left Twist
sl1 to CN and hold in front. p1, p1 from CN.

Purled Right Twist
sl1 to CN and hold in back. p1, p1 from CN.

c2 over 2 left
sl2 to CN, hold in front. k2, k2 from CN.

c2 over 2 right
sl2 to CN, hold in back. k2, k2 from CN.

c2 over 2 flex
Sock 1: sl2 to CN, hold in back. k2, k2 from CN.
Sock 2: sl2 to CN, hold in front. k2, k2 from CN.

CROSSING SOCKS

by Luise O'Neill

FINISHED MEASUREMENTS

7.75 (8.25, 8.75)" finished foot circumference; 11" high.

YARN

Knit Picks Stroll Tweed Sock Yarn
(65% Superwash Merino, 25% Nylon, 10% Donegal Tweed; 231 yards /50g): Garnet Heather 26283, 2 balls.

NEEDLES

US 1.5 (2.5mm) DPNs or two 24" circular needles for two circulars technique, or one 32" or longer circular needle for Magic Loop technique, or size to obtain gauge.

NOTIONS

Yarn Needle
Stitch Markers
Cable Needle
Scrap Yarn or Stitch Holder

GAUGE

32 sts and 42 rows = 4" in St st in the rnd, blocked.
30 sts = 4" over Chart B cable pattern in the rnd, blocked.

Notes:

The Crossing is a poignant ballad written and performed by Cape Breton's own Rita MacNeil; it speaks of the ocean crossings that so many undertook to start a new life across the sea and the ever-present yearnings for home. The cables in this pattern are perfect reminders of the intertwining journeys of these courageous individuals.

These toe-up socks begin with a wide toe. The cable pattern begins in a V-shape and grows to fill the instep while the sole is worked in Stockinette stitch. The repeat section in Chart C allows for adjustment of the leg height, if desired. The top of the leg is worked in a lattice pattern and ends in a rolled cuff.

This pattern is charted only. Begin reading charts at bottom right. All rows are RS rows and are read from right to left. Charts show the RS of the work at all times. The red border in Chart C identifies the repeat.

Judy's Magic Cast On: Tutorial on Knit Picks website can be found at http://tutorials.knitpicks.com/judys-magic-cast-on/.

Wrap and Turn (W&T): Tutorial on Knit Picks website can be found at http://tutorials.knitpicks.com/wptutorials/short-rows-wrap-and-turn-or-wt/.

DIRECTIONS

Toe

Using Judy's Magic Cast On, CO 20 sts (10 sts on each needle). Place an end of rnd M. Note: This CO includes 1 knit rnd; if your chosen CO does not include this, knit 1 rnd before working the following directions. Divide sts onto your preferred needle(s), if necessary.

An additional M is placed in the next rnd to mark the division between sole and instep sts.
Rnd 1 (Inc Rnd): KFB, K7, KFB, K1, PM, KFB, K7, KFB, K1. 24 sts.
Rnd 2 (Inc Rnd): *KFB, K to 2 sts before M, KFB, K1, SM; rep from *. 28 sts.
Rep Rnd 2 twice more. 32, then 36 sts.
Rnd 5: Knit.
Rnd 6 (Inc Rnd): Rep Rnd 2. 40 sts.
Rep Rnds 5-6 until there are 60 (64, 68) sts in total, 30 (32, 34) sts each for sole and instep.

Foot

Foot Rnd 1: K to M, SM, K1 (2, 3), work Chart A, K1 (2, 3).
Foot Rnd 2: K to M, SM, P1 (2, 3), work Chart A, P1 (2, 3).
Foot Rnds 3-30: Rep Foot Rnds 1-2.
Foot Rnd 31: K to M, SM, K1 (2, 3), work Chart B, K1 (2, 3).
Foot Rnd 32: K to M, SM, P1 (2, 3), work Chart B, P1 (2, 3).
Rep Foot Rnds 31-32 until sock measures 5 (6, 6.25)" or 3.25 (3.5, 3.75)" shorter than desired foot length.

Gusset

Two sts are increased every other rnd in this section to form the gusset. The instep sts continue in pattern until 2 full repeats of Chart B have been completed; note that the second repeat of Chart B will not be complete until part-way up the leg.

Gusset Rnd 1 (Inc Rnd): K2, M1R, K to last 2 sts before M, M1L, K2, SM, continue in pattern on instep sts. 2 sts inc.
Gusset Rnd 2: K to M, SM, continue in pattern on instep sts.
Rep Gusset Rnds 1-2 until there are 48 (50, 54) Sole sts ending having worked an Inc Rnd.

Heel

Turning the Heel

The instep sts will not be worked in this section; the 15 (16, 17) sts on either end of the sole section also will be set aside until after the heel is turned. The center 18 (18, 20) sts of the sole needle(s) form the base of the heel cap.
Heel Row 1 (RS – Inc Row): K15 (16, 17), place 15 (16, 17) sts just worked onto a stitch holder or scrap yarn, K1, KFB, K14 (14, 16), Sl2 to RH needle, place next 15 (16, 17) sts on stitch holder or scrap yarn, Sl2 back to LH needle, W&T. 19 (19, 21) sts on sole needle(s). Only these sts will be worked over the following rows.
Heel Row 2 (WS – Inc Row): Sl1 WYIF, PFB, P to last 2 sts, W&T. 1 st inc.
Heel Row 3 (Inc Row): Sl1, KFB, K to last 3 sts, W&T. 1 st inc.
Heel Row 4 (Inc Row): Sl1 WYIF, PFB, P to last 3 sts, W&T. 1 st inc.
Rep Rows 3-4 leaving 1 more st unworked for each set of rows e.g. on Heel Row 5 and 6 leave 4 sts unworked, on Heel

Row 7 and 8 leave 5 sts unworked, etc. until there are 30 (32, 34) sts on the sole needle(s).

The SSK and P2tog worked at the end of the next two rows form a small gap; this is the gap referred to in the following Heel Flap section. The SSK and P2tog dec use one st from either side of that gap.
Next Row (RS): Knitting any wraps along with their corresponding sts, Sl1, K to last st, Sl1 to RH needle, transfer 15 (16, 17) held sts onto LH needle, Sl1 back to LH needle, SSK. Turn. 1 st dec.
Next Row (WS): Purling any wraps along with their corresponding sts, Sl1 WYIF, P to last st, Sl1 WYIF to RH needle, transfer 15 (16, 17) held sts onto LH needle, Sl1 WYIF back to LH needle, P2tog. Turn. 1 st dec.

Heel Flap

The heel flap is worked in a slipped stitch pattern in which alternate sts are slipped WYIB on RS rows.
Heel Flap Row 1 (RS): Sl1, *K1, Sl1; rep from * to 1 st before gap, SSK (one st from either side of the gap). Turn. 1 st dec.
Heel Flap Row 2 (WS): Sl1 WYIF, P to 1 st before gap, P2tog (one st from either side of gap). Turn. 1 st dec.
Rep previous 2 rows until all previously held sts have been incorporated into the heel flap sts. Heel flap: 30 (32, 34) sts; total: 60 (64, 68) sts.

Leg

Knitting in the rnd resumes.

Next Rnd: Continue in pattern as set by instep sts, working pattern twice (once over the back leg sts and once over the front leg sts) until Chart B has been completed twice in total.
Next Rnd: K1 (2, 3), work Chart C, K2 (4, 6), work Chart C, K1 (2, 3).
Next Rnd: P1 (2, 3), work Chart C, P2 (4, 6), work Chart C, P1 (2, 3).
Rep previous two rnds until Chart C has been completed, then rep previous two rnds working only Rows 19-22 of Chart C until leg, from bottom of heel, measures approximately 8.25", or 2.75" shorter than desired height ending having completed a Row 22 of Chart C.
Next Rnd: K1 (2, 3), work Chart D, K2 (4, 6), work Chart D, K1 (2, 3).
Next Rnd: P1 (2, 3), work Chart D, P2 (4, 6), work Chart D, P1 (2, 3).
Rep previous two rnds until Chart D has been completed.

Cuff

Next Rnd: Knit.
Next Rnd: Purl.
Knit 6 rnds to form the roll-down cuff.

Bind off loosely. Cut yarn leaving a 6" tail.

Finishing

Weave in ends, wash and block.

Chart A

Legend

K — Knit stitch	Left Twist — sl1 to CN, hold in front. k1, k1 from CN.	Right Twist, purl bg — sl1 to CN, hold in back. k1, p1 from CN.	
P — Purl stitch	Right Twist — sl1 to CN, hold in back. k1, k1 from CN.	Purled Left Twist — sl1 to CN and hold in front. p1, p1 from CN.	
Pattern Repeat	Left Twist, purl bg — sl1 to CN, hold in front. p1, k1 from CN.	Purled Right Twist — sl1 to CN and hold in back. p1, p1 from CN.	

Chart B

28 27 26 25 24 23 22 21 20 19 18 17 16 15 14 13 12 11 10 9 8 7 6 5 4 3 2 1
62
61
60
59
58
57
56
55
54
53
52
51
50
49
48
47
46
45
44
43
42
41
40
39
38
37
36
35
34
33
32
31

Chart C

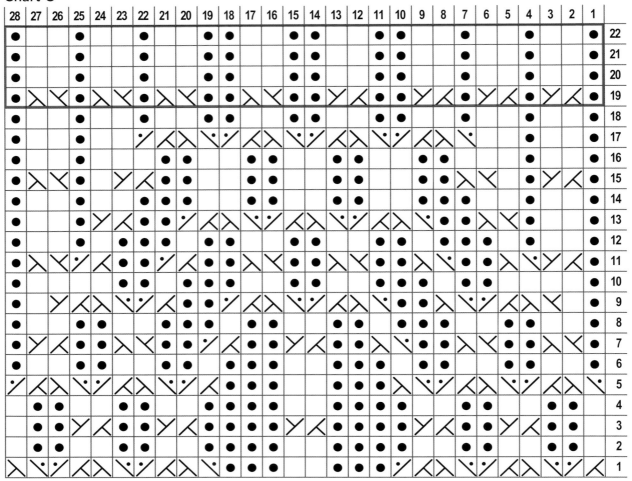

Chart D

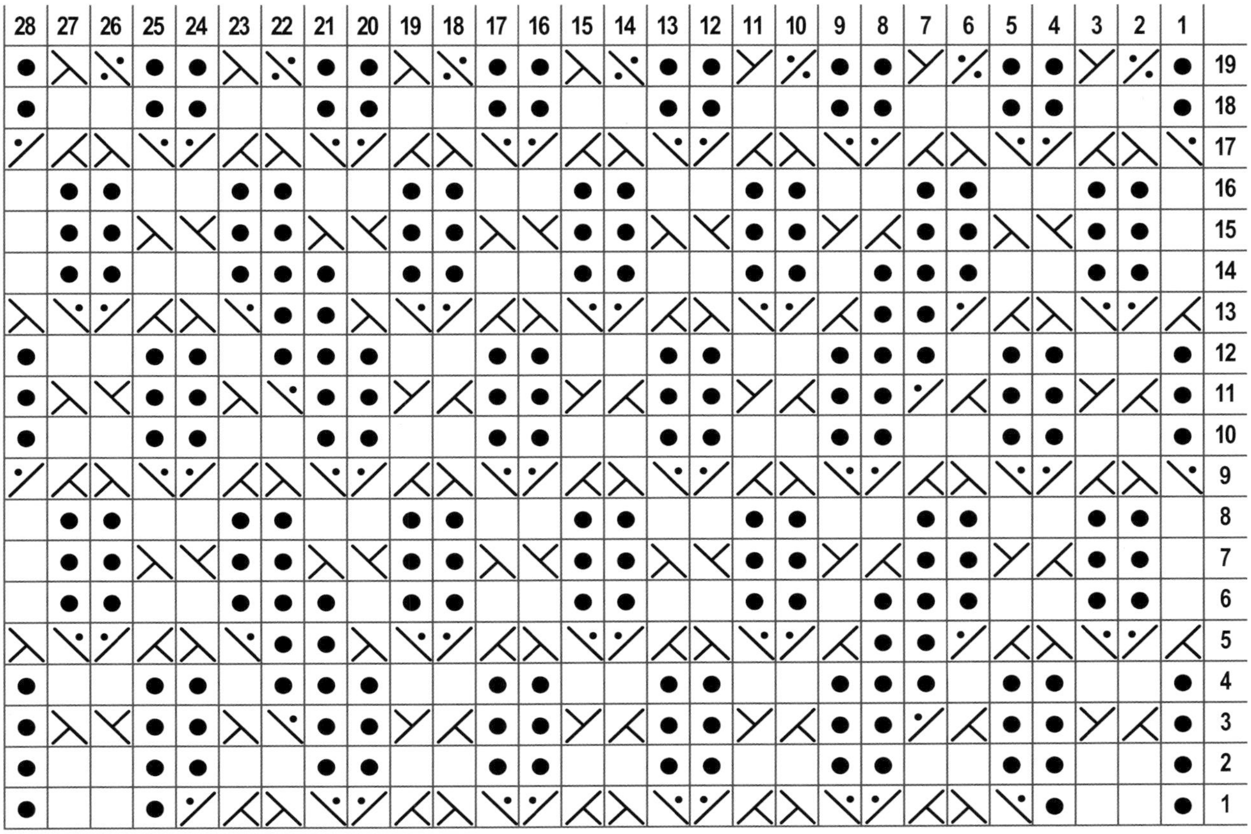

DON'T INTERRUPT SOCKS

by Megan Dial

FINISHED MEASUREMENTS

7.5" circumference x 8.5 (9.5, 10.5)" long from back of heel to tip of toe; to fit US women's shoe sizes 5-6.5 (7-9, 10-11)

YARN

Knit Picks Hawthorne Multi
(80% Superwash Fine Highland Wool, 20% Polyamide (Nylon); 357 yards/100g): Woodstock 27421, 1 skein.

NEEDLES

US 1 (2.25mm) DPNs, or size to obtain gauge.

NOTIONS

Yarn Needle
Stitch Markers

GAUGE

36 sts and 44 rows = 4" over Slip Stitch Pattern in the rnd, blocked.

Notes:

A uniquely constructed sock knit entirely in the round. No heel flap and gusset, no short rows, no afterthought, just clever shaping.

A fun slip stitch pattern on the top of the foot shortens the fabric to prevent bunching while a Stockinette back, heel, and bottom with clever increases and decreases makes plenty of room for a comfortable heel. This pattern is especially well-suited to striped and variegated yarns to show off the unbroken stripes around the heel and the fun "interruptions" on top.

Slip Stitch Pattern (in the rnd over 68 sts)
Rnd 1: K10, P2, K2, P2, *K2, Sl1, K2, P1; rep from * 5 more times, P1, K2, P2, K11.
Rep Rnd 1 once.
Rnd 2: K10, P2, K2, P2, ***K5, P1; rep from * 5 more times,** P1, K2, P2, K11.

Special Note on Measurements
ALL measurements need to be taken from the BACK of the sock (St st section) for accurate construction. The front of the leg and top of the foot will be shorter by nature of the slipped stitch pattern. This is to avoid disproportionate fabric on the top of the foot. Take all length measurements on the back of the leg and bottom of the foot.

For a video demonstration of how to work Kitchener St, see http://tutorials.knitpicks.com/wptutorials/kitchener-stitch/.

DIRECTIONS

Cuff
CO 68 sts. Arrange on 4 DPNs with 16, 18, 18, 16 sts on Needles 1-4 respectively, PM, and join in the rnd, being careful not to twist sts.

Rib Rnd: *K1 TBL, P1; rep from * to end.
Rep Rib Rnd for 15 more rnds.

Leg
K 4 rnds.
Work Slip Stitch Pattern until piece measures 5" from CO edge.

Heel
Continue working in the rnd with front of leg/top of foot in Slip Stitch Pattern as established on Needles 2 and 3, while working Heel Pattern on Needles 1 and 4.

Heel Setup Rnd
Needle 1: K10, P2, K2, P2; Needles 2 and 3: Work Slip Stitch Pattern as established; Needle 4: P1, K2, P2, K3, PM, K8.

Continue to work Needles 2 and 3 as established while working the following:
Rnd 1: Needle 1: K7, M1L, K to last 6 sts, P2, K2, P2; Needle 4: P1, K2, P2, K to M, M1R, SM, K to end. 2 sts inc.
Rnd 2: Needle 1: K to last 6 sts, P2, K2, P2; Needle 4: P1, K2, P2, K to M, SM, K to end.
Rep Rnds 1 and 2 nine more times. 88 sts.
Then work Rnd 2 four times.

Continue to work Needles 2 and 3 as established while working the following:
Rnd 3: Needle 1: K7, SSK, K to last 6 sts, P2, K2, P2; Needle 4: P1, K2, P2, K to 2 sts before M, K2tog, SM, K to end. 2 sts dec.
Rnd 4: Needle 1: K to last 6 sts, P2, K2, P2; Needle 4: P1, K2, P2, K to M, SM, K to end.
Repeat Rnds 3 and 4 nine more times. 68 sts.

Foot
Work evenly in Slip Stitch Pattern as established until foot measures approximately 7.25 (8.25, 9.25)" from back of heel *on bottom of foot.*

Dec Rnd: Needles 1 and 3: K to last 3 sts, K2tog, K1; Needles 2 and 4: K1, SSK, K to end of needle. 4 sts dec.
Knit evenly, repeating Dec Rnd every 4th rnd once, every 3rd rnd twice, every 2nd rnd twice, then every rnd 3 times. 32 sts.

Final Dec Rnd: K6, K2tog, SSK, K12, K2tog, SSK, K6. 28 sts.

Finishing
K to end of Needle 1. Sl all sts from Needle 4 to Needle 1 and from Needle 3 to Needle 2. Break yarn leaving a tail of approximately 24" for finishing. Thread tail through yarn needle and use the Kitchener Stitch technique to graft remaining sts together neatly.

Weave in ends, wash and block.

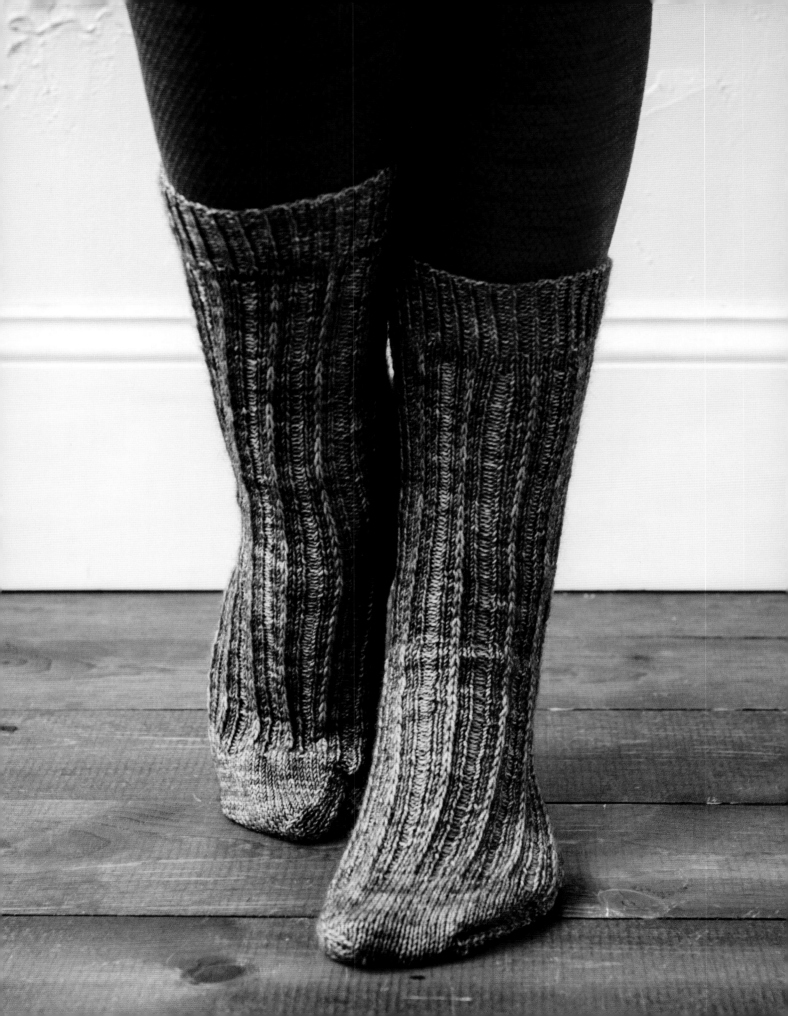

EASY REPEAT SOCKS

by Aud Bergo

FINISHED MEASUREMENTS

Foot circumference 8.25" unstretched; foot length from back of heel to tip of toe 10" adjustable; leg length including cuff and heel flap 9.25"; to fit US women's shoe sizes 7.5 - 9.

YARN

Knit Picks Stroll Sock Yarn
(75% Superwash Merino Wool, 25% Nylon; 231 yards/50g): MC Navy 23694, 2 balls.
Knit Picks Stroll Tonal Sock Yarn
(75% Superwash Merino Wool, 25% Nylon; 462 yards/100g): C1 Cordial 27064, 1 skein.

NEEDLES

US 1 (2.25mm) 24" circular needles for two circulars technique, or one 32" or longer circular needle for Magic Loop technique. Size to obtain gauge.
US 2 (2.75mm) 24" circular needles for two circulars technique, or one 32" or longer circular needle for Magic Loop technique. Size to obtain gauge.

NOTIONS

Yarn Needle
Stitch Markers (optional)

GAUGE

34 sts and 42 rows = 4" over Chart A in the rnd on larger needles, blocked.

Notes:
The Easy Repeat Socks are top down socks knitted in the round. They have a heel flap and gusset decrease. The pattern gives flexible socks that shape well around the foot. Shaft and foot length can be adjusted by increasing or decreasing the number of repeating rows.

The description is written for knitting with 2 circular needles. Needle 1 for the back of leg, heel, gusset and sole, and Needle 2 for the front of leg and instep. Alternatively, use Magic Loop technique or DPN's.

The pattern has an 8 st repeat over 4 rows apart from center part on back of leg. Rounds 1 and 3 are identical. For Round 2 a contrast color with hand painted yarn is used to give an extra color dimension to the pattern. The sole has knit and purl sts only. The right and left socks are identical and the rounds starts with Needle 1.

All charts are knitted in the round. Work each chart row from the right to the left as a RS row, with the color on each st as shown. The cuff, heel and toe are knitted with the main color only.

Knit One Under Loose Strand (K1 ULS): Knit 1 under loose strand from 2 rnds earlier by inserting needle under loose strand and into next st K-wise, from front to back. Knit st and bring the new st out from under the strand.

Ribbed Pattern (in the rnd over an even number of sts)
All Rnds: (K1, P1) to end.

DIRECTIONS

Before you start, cut off two 23" loose threads of MC to be used for picking up sts on the Heel Flap.

Cuff

With MC CO 66 sts on larger circular needle.
Begin Ribbed Pattern, and at the same time distribute sts onto two smaller circular needles with 33 sts on each. Join to work in the round, being careful not to twist sts.
Work in Ribbed Pattern for 2".
Next Rnd: K in the round, inc 2 sts evenly on each needle. 70 sts, 35 sts on each needle.

Leg

Change to larger needles. Work both of the Chart A Leg Rnds 1-4 fifteen times, or until the leg measures approximately 6.5" from CO.
When the leg is finished both MC and C1 yarns are at the end of Needle 2.

Heel

The heel is knitted back and forth on Needle 1 with MC.

Heel Flap (worked flat)

Set Up Row (RS): K across, inc 1 st to 36 sts.
Heel Flap Row 1 (WS): Sl1, P remaining sts.
Heel Flap Row 2 (RS): (Sl1, K1) 18 times.
Rep these 2 rows 16 times more, 34 rows total, or until the flap measures 2.5-2.75".

Turn the Heel (worked flat)

Row 1 (WS): Sl1, P20, P2tog, P1, turn work. 1 st dec.
Row 2 (RS): Sl1, K7, SSK, K1, turn work. 1 st dec.
Row 3: Sl1, P to one st before gap, P2tog, P1, turn work. 1 st dec.
Row 4: Sl1, K to one st before gap, SSK, K1, turn work. 1 st dec.
Rep Rows 3 and 4 until all sts have been worked. 22 heel flap sts.

Gusset

With the RS facing you and MC, PU and K 17 sts evenly on the left side of the heel flap using the MC thread at the end of Needle 1. Arrange the picked up sts and heel sts to get ready to PU and K sts on the right side of the heel flap. Start on the instep corner, and with the loose 23" thread PU and K 17 sts evenly. Leave the loose thread and arrange all 56 sts on Needle 1, 17 st on left side of heel flap, 22 sts across heel flap, 17 sts on right side of heel flap.
Next Row (WS): Sl 1, P across and dec 1 st centered on the heel flap. 55 sts.
MC and C1 threads are now in position for Needle 1 to start working Chart B Gusset Decrease.

Gusset Decrease

Resume working in the rnd.
Rnd 1: Needle 1: Work Chart B Gusset Decrease Rnd 1; Needle 2: Work Chart A Needle 2 chart Rnd 1 across Instep.
Rnd 2: Needle 1: SSK first 2 sts as shown on chart Rnd 2, K and P as shown on chart to last 2 sts, K2tog as shown on chart. Needle 2: Work Chart A Needle 2 chart Rnd 2.
Cont to work as established, repeating Rnds 1-4 of Chart A Needle 2, until Chart B is finished and sts on Needle 1 are dec to 35 sts, 70 sts total.

Foot

Next Row: Needle 1: Work Chart C Foot Rnd 1 over the 35 Sole sts. Needle 2: Work Chart A Needle 2 Rnd 1 over the 35 instep sts.
Cont in pattern as established, rep Rows 1-4 of charts until foot measures 1.5" less than desired length, ending with Rnd 1 or 4. Cut C1.

Shaping the Toe

Change to smaller needles. With MC work Chart D Shaping the Toe for both needles. These are:
Rnds 1-2: Needles 1 and 2: K all sts.
Rnd 3: Needles 1 and 2: K1, SSK, K to last 3 sts on needle, K2tog, K1; rep from * for Needle 2. 4 sts dec.
Rnd 4: Needles 1 and 2: K all sts.
Rep Rnds 3-4 two more times. 58 sts.
Rep Rnd 3, 11 times. 14 sts.

Cut the yarn and pull the thread through the remaining sts. Use a needle to secure the thread and sew the hole on the toe tip.

Finishing

Weave in ends, wash and block to finished measurements. Make second sock identically.

Chart A Leg Front (Needle 2)

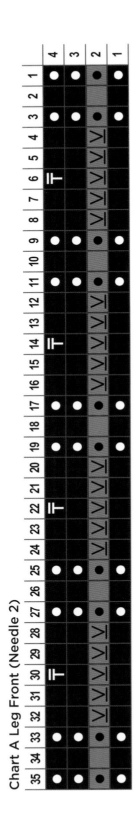

Chart A Leg Back (Needle 1)

Legend

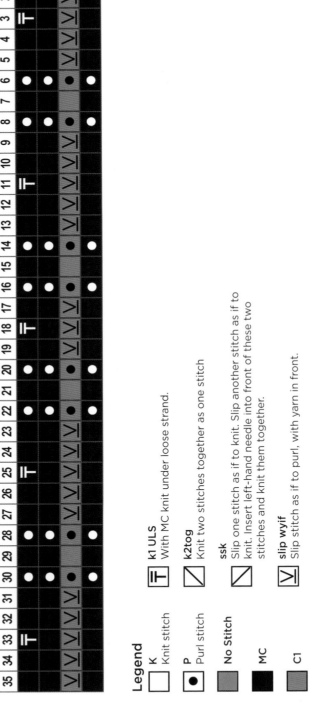

	K	Knit stitch
●	P	Purl stitch
		No Stitch
		MC
		C1

	k1 ULS	With MC knit under loose strand.
	k2tog	Knit two stitches together as one stitch
	ssk	Slip one stitch as if to knit. Slip another stitch as if to knit. Insert left-hand needle into front of these two stitches and knit them together.
	slip wyif	Slip stitch as if to purl, with yarn in front.

Chart B Gusset Decreases

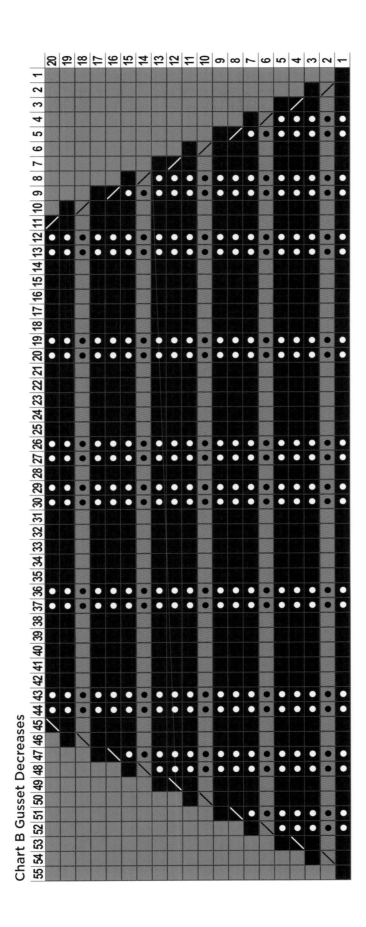

Chart C Foot

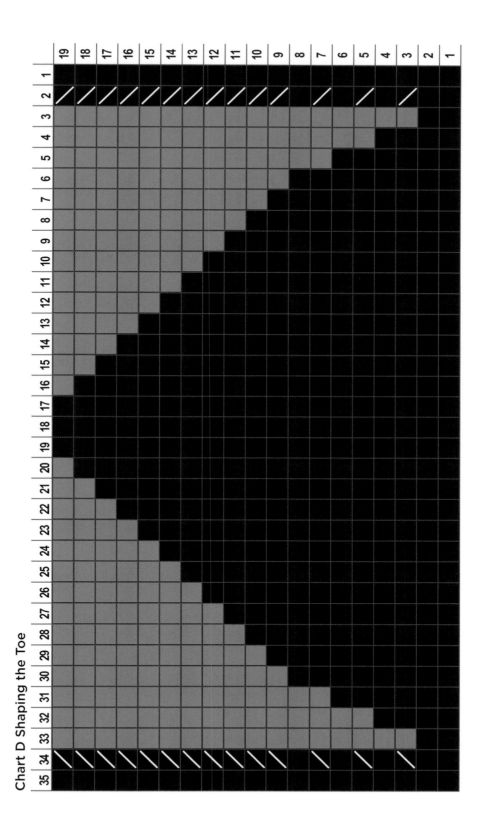

Chart D Shaping the Toe

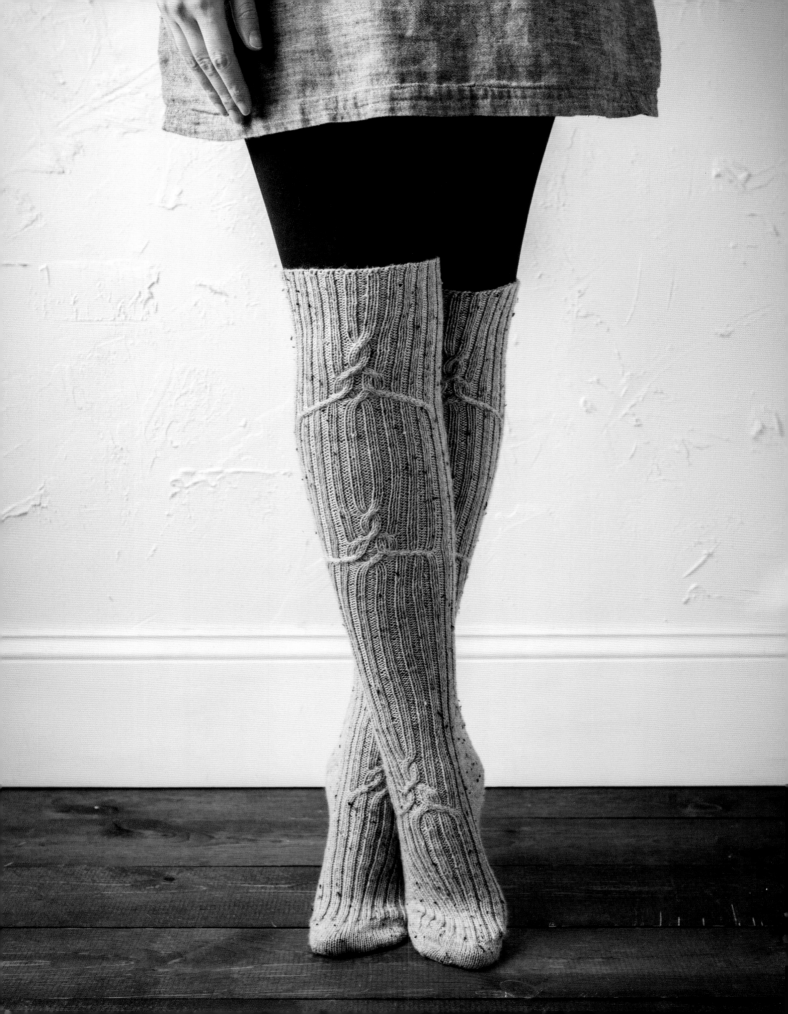

FONTANA SOCKS

by Cheryl Toy

FINISHED MEASUREMENTS

6.75 (7.5, 8.5)" foot circumference, 20" in length from sole.

YARN

Knit Picks Stroll Tweed Sock Yarn
(65% Superwash Merino Wool, 25% Nylon, 10% Donegal; 231 yards/50g): Down Heather 26296, 6 balls.

NEEDLES

US 1 (2.5mm) DPNs or two 24" circular needles for two circulars technique, or one 32" or longer circular needle for Magic Loop technique, or size to obtain gauge.

NOTIONS

Yarn Needle

6 Stitch Markers; 1 distinctive, 2 removable

Cable Needle

GAUGE

36 sts and 48 rows = 4" in 2 X 2 Ribbing in the rnd, blocked.

Notes:

Long and ribbed, these over-the-knee socks make a perfect showcase for a solid, kettle-dyed tonal or a subtle gradient. A cascading cable flows over long stretches of sinuous ribbing, incorporating extra ribs as the socks grow wider. Fontana Socks feature the super easy Fleegle Heel, so color changes track organically around the foot while the simple ribbing ensures a fabulous fit from ankle to thigh.

Socks are worked from the toe up using a Fleegle heel. Cable stitches and increases are worked into ribbing pattern as the socks grow wider.

Charts are worked in the round, read each row from right to left as a RS row.

Judy's Magic Cast On tutorial can be found here: http://tutorials.knitpicks.com/judys-magic-cast-on/.

2 X 2 Ribbing A (in the rnd over multiples of 4 sts)
All Rnds: *K2, P2; rep from * to end of rnd.
Where there are not enough sts to end P2, end as K2.

2 X 2 Ribbing B (in the rnd over multiples of 4 sts)
All Rnds: *P2, K2; rep from * to end of rnd.
Where there are not enough sts to end K2, end as P2.

Make 1 Left-leaning Stitch (M1L):
With left needle tip, lift strand between needles from front to back. Knit the lifted loop through the back.

Make 1 Right-leaning Stitch (M1R):
With left needle tip, lift strand between needles from back to front. Knit the lifted loop through the front.

Lifted Increase (LI-K):
Lift the st from the row below the first st on the left needle, placing on the left needle. Knit the st.

Lifted Increase (LI-P):
Lift the st from the row below the first st on the left needle, placing on the left needle. Purl the st.

SDM: Side marker.
PSDM: Place side marker.
MM: Motif marker.
PMM: Place motif marker.
RM: Removable marker.
PRM: Place removable marker.
PC: Purl column.
KC: Knit column.

DIRECTIONS

Toe

Using the Judy's Magic method, CO 28 (36, 44) sts divided evenly over 2 needle tips. Work 1 rnd even, PM (distinctive) for beginning of rnd, PSDM after 14 (18, 22) sts. Inc Rnd: *K1, M1R, K to 1 st before SDM, M1L, K1; rep from * once more. 4 sts inc. Work Inc Rnd every other rnd a total of 8 times to 60 (68, 76) sts.

Foot

Sizes 6.75" and 8.5": Work in 2 X 2 Ribbing A to SDM (these will be the instep sts), K to end of rnd (these will be the sole sts).
Size 7.5": Work in 2 X 2 Ribbing B to SDM, K to end of rnd.
All Sizes: Cont in pattern until work measures 7 (7.5, 8.25)" from tip of toe, or until work reaches point where top of instep meets ankle when the foot is fully flexed.

On last rnd, PMM after first 4 (6, 8) sts, work 22 sts in pattern, PMM, work in pattern to end of rnd.

Heel Shaping

Inc Rnd: Work in 2 X 2 Ribbing to MM, SM, work Chart A between MMs, SM, work in 2 X 2 Ribbing to SDM, SM, K1, M1L, K to 1 st before next M, M1R, K1. 2 sole sts inc. Cont to work Chart A across instep sts while working an Inc Rnd every other rnd across sole sts another 13 (15, 17) times, until there are 58 (66, 74) sole sts.

Turn Heel

The heel is turned using short rows which are worked back and forth across the sole sts. The instep sts will remain unworked during this section.

PRM after 29 (33, 37) sts.
Setup Row 1 (RS): K to RM, SM, K2, SSK, K1, turn. 1 st dec.
Setup Row 2 (WS): Sl the first st, P to M, SM, P2, P2tog, P1, turn. 1 st dec.
A gap will develop on either side of the heel where the work has been turned. This gap acts as a visual reminder of where to turn the short rows, thus no counting is necessary. Proceed with short rows as follows:
Short Row 1 (RS): Sl first st, K to 1 st before the gap (short row is turned across the gap), SSK, K1, turn. 1 st dec.
Short Row 2 (WS): Sl first st, P to 1 st before the gap, P2tog, P1, turn. 1 st dec. Cont to rep Short Rows 1-2 until last possible short row has been worked on the RS.
There is one more short row to work on the WS, but do not turn and work that short row now. Rather, PRM around the sts and across the gap. Those sts will be worked as a K2tog on the next full rnd.

Leg

Resume working in the rnd, cont in pattern to SDM, SM, K2tog (these are the marked sts), K to end of rnd. 60 (68, 76) sts.
Sizes 6.75" and 8.5": Cont in pattern to SDM, SM, work 2 X 2 Ribbing B across remaining sts.
Size 7.5": Cont in pattern to SDM, SM, work 2 X 2 Ribbing A across remaining sts.
All Sizes: Cont in this manner through Rnd 23 of Chart A.
Next Rnd: Work in pattern to MM, remove MM, work Rnd 24 of Chart A, remove MM, work in pattern to SDM, SM, cont in pattern to end of rnd.
Rep last rnd until work measures 7" from RM at heel turn.

First Leg Increase

Rnd 1: Work in pattern to SDM, SM, LI-P in center of second purl column (PC), work in pattern to next PC, LI-P in center of PC, work in pattern to last 3 PC, LI-P in center of PC, work in pattern to next PC, LI-P in center of PC, work in pattern to end of rnd. 4 sts inc. 64 (72, 80) sts.

Rnd 2: Work in pattern to SDM, remove M, work 1 st in pattern, PSDM, work in pattern to end of rnd, remove M for beginning of rnd and place it before last st worked. Sts are now evenly divided over needles.

Work in pattern for 24 rnds, then work Rnds 1-2 of First Leg Increase. 68 (76, 84) sts.

Next Rnd: Work 2 (4, 6) sts in pattern, PMM, work Chart B over next 30 sts, PMM, work in pattern to end of rnd. Cont in pattern through Rnd 4 of Chart B.

Next Rnd: Work in pattern to MM, remove MM, K2, P2, PMM, work Chart A over next 22 sts, PMM, P2, K2, remove MM, work in pattern to end of rnd.
Cont in this manner through Rnd 23 of Chart A.
Next Rnd: Work in pattern to MM, remove MM, work Rnd 24 of Chart A, remove MM, work in pattern to SDM, SM, cont in pattern to end of rnd.

Work Rnds 1-2 of First Leg Increase. 72 (80, 88) sts.
Work 12 rnds in Ribbing pattern.

Second Leg Increase

Rnd 1: Work in pattern to SDM, SM, LI-K in center of KC (knit column), work in pattern to next KC, LI-K in center of KC, work in pattern to last 3 KC, LI-K in center of KC, work in pattern to next KC, LI-K in center of KC, work in pattern to end of rnd. 4 sts inc. 76 (84, 92) sts.
Rnd 2: Work in pattern to SDM, remove SDM, work 1 st in pattern, PSDM, work in pattern to end of rnd, remove M for beginning of rnd and place it before last st worked. Sts are now evenly divided over needles.

Work 12 rnds in Ribbing pattern, then work Rnds 1-2 of Second Leg Increase. 80 (88, 96) sts.

Next Rnd: Work 1 (3, 5) sts in pattern, PMM, work Chart C over next 38 sts, PMM, work in pattern to end of rnd. Cont in pattern through Rnd 4 of Chart C.

Next Rnd: Work in pattern to MM, remove MM, K2, P2, PMM, work Chart B over next 30 sts, PMM, P2, K2, remove MM, work in pattern to SDM, work in pattern to end of rnd. Cont in pattern through Rnd 4 of Chart B.

Next Rnd: Work in pattern to MM, SMM, (K2, P2) twice, work Chart A over next 22 sts, (P2, K2) twice, SMM, work in pattern to SDM, work in pattern to end of rnd. Cont in pattern through Rnd 24 of Chart A, then work in Ribbing pattern for 2.5" or desired length. BO loosely in pattern.

Finishing

Weave in ends, wash and block to dimensions.

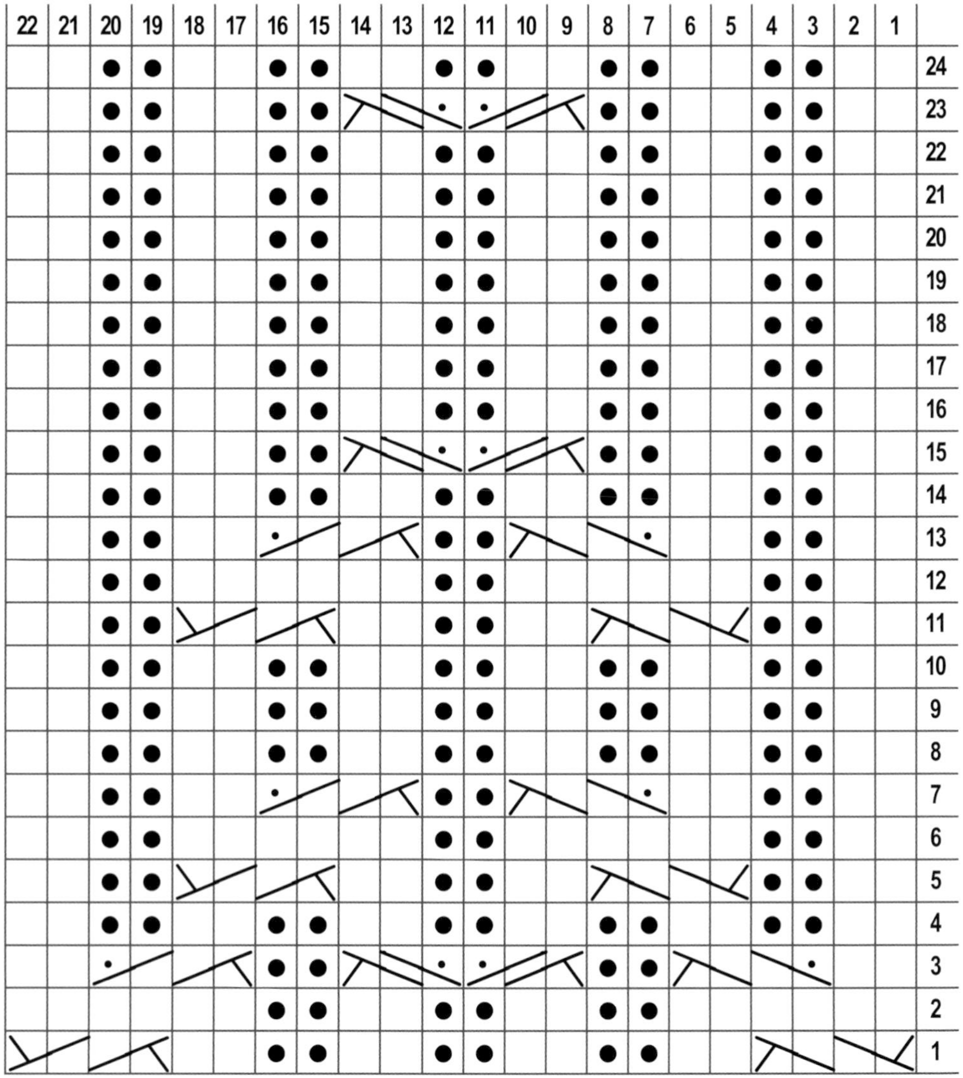

Legend

K
Knit stitch

P
Purl stitch

c1 over 2 left P
sl1 to CN, hold in front. p2, k1 from CN.

c1 over 2 right P
sl2 to CN, hold in back. k1, p2 from CN.

c2 over 2 left
sl2 to CN, hold in front. k2, k2 from CN.

c2 over 2 right
sl2 to CN, hold in back. k2, k2 from CN.

c2 over 2 left P
sl2 to CN, hold in front. p2, k2 from CN.

c2 over 2 right P
sl2 to CN, hold in back. k2, p2 from CN.

Chart A

Chart B

Chart C

LORENTZ

by M K Nance

FINISHED MEASUREMENTS

6.75 (7.75, 8.75, 9.75)" foot
circumference; foot length is adjustable.

YARN

Knit Picks Hawthorne Tonal Hand Paint
(80% Superwash Fine Highland
Wool, 20% Polyamide (Nylon); 357
yards/100g): Sweet Home 27409, 1 skein.

NEEDLES

US 0 (2mm) DPNs or two 24" circular
needles for two circulars technique, or one
32" or longer circular needle for Magic
Loop technique, or size to obtain gauge.

NOTIONS

Yarn Needle
Stitch Markers
Cable Needle

GAUGE

36 sts and 50 rnds = 4" in St st in the
rnd, blocked.

For pattern support, contact
mknanceknit@gmail.com

Notes:

Lorentz was a collaborator of Einstein on the Theory of Special Relativity. This pattern was inspired by half watching a Khan Academy video about Special Relativity and the Lorentz Transformation.

When working charts in the rnd, read each row from right to left as a RS row.

Wrap and Turn

Work until the st to be wrapped. If knitting: Bring the yarn to the front of the work, Sl next st as if to purl, return the yarn to the back; turn work and slip wrapped st onto the RH needle. Continue across the row. If purling: Bring yarn to the back of work, Sl next st as if to purl, return the yarn to the front; turn work and slip wrapped st onto RH needle. Continue across the row.

Picking up Wraps

Work to the wrapped st. If knitting, insert the RH needle under the wrap, then through the wrapped st K-wise. Knit the st and the wrap together. If purling, Sl the wrapped st P-wise onto the RH needle, and use the LH needle to lift the wrap and place them on the RH needle. Sl the wrap and st back on the LH needle and purl tog.

Turkish CO Method

Make a slip knot and place it on one needle. Place 2 needles parallel, one on top of the other, with pointed ends facing the same direction and with slip knot loop on bottom needle. Take yarn and wrap around back, over the top and back to the front, looping around both needles. Make each loop to the right of the last loop. Repeat until there are enough loops for half your needed CO sts, minus 1. Wrap yarn around the top needle once more and bring the yarn between the needles. With another needle, knit the sts on the top needle, then knit the sts on the bottom needle. If using circulars, you can pull the bottom needle through the loops so the loops are now on the cable and use it to knit the loops on the top needle.

Lorentz 6.75" (worked in the rnd over 29 sts)

Rnd 1: (K1, P2, K3, P3, K3, P2) x 2, K1.
Rnd 2: K1, P1, (K3, P3) x 2, K1, (P3, K3) x 2, P1, K1.
Rnd 3: K1, P1, K2, P3, K3, P4, K1, P4, K3, P3, K2, P1, K1.
Rnd 4: (K1, P1, K1, P3, K3, P3, K1, P1) x 2, K1.
Rnd 5: K1, P4, K3, P3, K2, P1, K1, P1, K2, P3, K3, P4, K1.
Rnd 6: K1, (P3, K3) x 2, P1, K1, P1, (K3, P3) x 2, K1.
Rep Rnds 1-6 for pattern.

Lorentz 7.75" (worked in the rnd over 33 sts)

Rnd 1: K1, P4, K3, P3, K3, P2, K1, P2, K3, P3, K3, P4, K1.
Rnd 2: (K1, [P3, K3] x 2, P3) x 2, K1.
Rnd 3: K1, P2, K3, P3, K3, P4, K1, P4, K3, P3, K3, P2, K1.
Rnd 4: K1, P1, (K3, P3) x 2, (K1, P1) x 2, K1, (P3, K3) x 2, P1 K1.
Rnd 5: (K1, P1, K2, P3, K3, P3, K2, P1) x 2, K1.
Rnd 6: K1, P1, K1, (P3, K3) x 2, P1, K1, P1, (K3, P3) x 2, K1, P1, K1.
Rep Rnds 1-6 for pattern.

Lorentz 8.75" (worked in the rnd over 37 sts)

Rnd 1: K1, P1, K2, (P3, K3) x 2, P2, K1, P2, (K3, P3) x 2, K2, P1, K1.
Rnd 2: K1, P1, (K1, [P3, K3] x 2, P3) x 2, K1, P1, K1.
Rnd 3: (K1, P4, K3, P3, K3, P4) x 2, K1.
Rnd 4: K1, (P3, K3) x 2, P3, (K1, P1) x 2, K1, (P3, K3) x 2, P3, K1.
Rnd 5: K1, P2, (K3, P3) x 2, K2, P1, K1, P1, K2, (P3, K3) x 2, P2, K1.
Rnd 6: (K1, P1, [K3, P3] x 2, K3, P1) x 2, K1.
Rep Rnds 1-6 for pattern.

Lorentz 9.75" (worked in the rnd over 41 sts)

Rnd 1: (K1, P2, [K3, P3] x 2, K3, P2) x 2, K1.
Rnd 2: K1, P1, (K3, P3) x 3, K1, (P3, K3) x 3, P1, K1.
Rnd 3: K1, P1, K2, (P3, K3) x 2, P4, K1, P4, (K3, P3) x 2, K2, P1, K1.
Rnd 4: (K1, P1, K1, [P3, K3] x 2, P3, K1, P1) x 2, K1.
Rnd 5: K1, P4, (K3, P3) x 2, K2, P1, K1, P1, K2, (P3, K3) x 2, P4, K1.
Rnd 6: K1, (P3, K3) x 3, P1, K1, P1, (K3, P3) x 3, K1.
Rep Rnds 1-6 for pattern.

DIRECTIONS

Toe

Using the Turkish method, CO 26 (30, 34, 38) sts. 13 (15, 17, 19) sts. PM and join to work in the rnd.

Inc Rnd: *K1, M1, K11 (13, 15, 17), M1, K1; PM rep from * once more. 30 (34, 38, 42) sts total, 15 (17, 19, 21) sts each for the instep and sole.
Next Rnd: Knit.
Inc Rnd: *K1, M1, K to 1 st before M, M1, K1, SM; rep from * once more. 4 sts inc.
Rep last 2 rnds 6 (7, 8, 9) more times, 58 (66, 74, 82) total sts, 29 (33, 37, 41) sts each for instep and sole.

Foot

Next Rnd: Work in Lorentz pattern for correct size, SM, K29 (33, 37, 41).
Work in pattern as established until piece measures 2.5" less than desired foot length.

Gusset

Inc Rnd: Work instep sts in pattern, SM, K1, M1, K to last st, M1, K1. 2 sts inc.
Next Rnd: Work instep sts in pattern, SM, K to the end.
Rep last 2 rnds 9 (10, 11, 12) more times. 78 (88, 98, 108) total sts, 29 (33, 37, 41) instep sts, and 49 (55, 61, 67) sole sts.

Turn Heel

Next Rnd: Work instep sts in pattern, SM. Heel turn is now worked back and forth in rows over sole sts.
Shape heel, using short-rows as follows:
Short Row 1 (RS): K33 (37, 41, 44), KFB, K1, W&T. 1 st inc.
Short Row 2 (WS): P20 (22, 24, 26), PFB, p1, W&T. 1 st inc.
Short Row 3: K to 5 sts before previously wrapped st, KFB, K1, W&T. 1 st inc.
Short Row 4: P to 5 sts before previously wrapped st, PFB, K1, W&T. 1 st inc.
Rep Short Rows 3 and 4 twice more. 57 (63, 69, 75) sole sts, with 4 wrapped sts at each side.
Next Rnd: With RS facing, K to end of sole sts, PU wrapped sts, then work instep sts in pattern.

Heel Flap

Row 1 (RS): K42 (47, 52, 55), PU wrapped sts, SSK, turn. 1 st dec.
Row 2 (WS): Sl 1, P27 (31, 35, 39), P2tog, turn. 1 st dec.
Row 3: (Sl 1, K1) 14 (16, 18, 20) times, SSK, turn. 1 st dec.
Rep Rows 2-3 12 (13, 14, 15) more times, then work Row 2 once more. 29 (33, 37, 41) heel sts remain. 58 (66, 74, 82) total sts.

Leg

Next Rnd: Work in Lorentz pattern for correct size, SM, and work in Lorentz pattern for correct size. Work as established until leg measures 5", or 1.5" less than desired length, ending on a Lorentz pattern Row 5 or 6.

Cuff

Next Rnd: Rep Rnd 6 of Lorentz pattern to create rib pattern for Cuff. Work as established for 1.5", or until sock measures desired length.
BO loosely.

Finishing

Weave in ends, wash and block. Repeat instructions for second sock.

Legend

☐	K — Knit stitch
⬛●	P — Purl stitch

Lorentz 6.75"

	29	28	27	26	25	24	23	22	21	20	19	18	17	16	15	14	13	12	11	10	9	8	7	6	5	4	3	2	1
6		●	●	●				●	●	●				●		●				●	●	●				●	●	●	
5		●	●	●	●				●	●	●			●		●			●	●	●				●	●	●	●	
4		●		●	●	●				●	●	●		●		●		●	●	●				●	●	●		●	
3		●			●	●	●				●	●	●	●		●	●	●	●				●	●	●			●	
2		●				●	●	●				●	●	●		●	●	●				●	●	●				●	
1		●	●				●	●	●				●	●		●	●				●	●	●				●	●	

Lorentz 7.75"

	33	32	31	30	29	28	27	26	25	24	23	22	21	20	19	18	17	16	15	14	13	12	11	10	9	8	7	6	5	4	3	2	1
6		●		●	●	●				●	●	●				●		●				●	●	●				●	●	●		●	
5		●			●	●	●				●	●	●			●		●			●	●	●				●	●	●			●	
4		●				●	●	●				●	●	●		●		●		●	●	●				●	●	●				●	
3		●	●				●	●	●				●	●	●	●		●	●	●	●				●	●	●					●	
2		●	●	●				●	●	●				●	●	●		●	●	●				●	●	●					●	●	
1		●	●	●	●				●	●	●				●	●		●	●				●	●	●				●	●	●	●	

Lorentz 8.75"

	1	2	3	4	5	6	7	8	9	10	11	12	13	14	15	16	17	18	19	20	21	22	23	24	25	26	27	28	29	30	31	32	33	34	35	36	37
6		●				●	●	●				●	●	●				●		●				●	●	●				●	●	●				●	
5		●	●				●	●	●				●	●	●			●		●			●	●	●				●	●	●				●	●	
4		●	●	●				●	●	●				●	●	●		●		●		●	●	●				●	●	●				●	●	●	
3		●	●	●	●				●	●	●				●	●	●	●		●	●	●	●				●	●	●				●	●	●	●	
2		●		●	●	●				●	●	●				●	●	●		●	●	●				●	●	●				●	●	●		●	
1		●			●	●	●				●	●	●				●	●		●	●				●	●	●				●	●	●			●	

Lorentz 9.75"

	1	2	3	4	5	6	7	8	9	10	11	12	13	14	15	16	17	18	19	20	21	22	23	24	25	26	27	28	29	30	31	32	33	34	35	36	37	38	39	40	41
6		●	●	●				●	●	●				●	●	●				●		●				●	●	●				●	●	●				●	●	●	
5		●	●	●	●				●	●	●				●	●	●			●		●			●	●	●				●	●	●				●	●	●	●	
4		●		●	●	●				●	●	●				●	●	●		●		●		●	●	●				●	●	●				●	●	●		●	
3		●			●	●	●				●	●	●				●	●	●	●		●	●	●	●				●	●	●				●	●	●			●	
2		●				●	●	●				●	●	●				●	●	●		●	●	●				●	●	●				●	●	●				●	
1		●	●				●	●	●				●	●	●				●	●		●	●				●	●	●				●	●	●				●	●	

PUGET SOUND SOCKS

by Allison Griffith

FINISHED MEASUREMENTS

7 (7.5, 8, 8.5, 9)" foot and leg circumference; sock is meant to be worn with zero or slight negative ease.

YARN

Knit Picks Capretta Yarn
(80% Fine Merino Wool, 10% Cashmere, 10% Nylon; 230 yards/50g): Shoal 27244, 2 balls.

NEEDLES

US 2 (2.75mm) DPNs, or size to obtain gauge.

NOTIONS

Yarn Needle
Stitch Marker (a split marker or safety pin is recommended)

GAUGE

30 sts and 39 rows = 4" in St st in the rnd, blocked.

Notes:
Puget Sound Socks are inspired by the gentle waves lapping at the shore of the beaches around Seattle. These socks are cozy enough to wear with your rubber boots, while searching the shore for sea glass and starfish, but cute enough that you'll want to show them off.

These socks are worked in the round from the top down. The left and right socks are mirrors of one another, with mirrored lace panels worked up the front, outside quadrant of each leg. The reinforced heel flap is worked with slipped stitches and short rows. Then, the established pattern is continued down the foot to right before the toe. The toe is worked plain, and closed up with the Kitchener Stitch.

The charts are worked in the round, read each row from right to left as a RS row.

2x2 Rib Pattern (in the rnd over a multiple of 4 sts)
All Rnds: (K2, P2) around.

Kitchener Stitch
Follow the instructions provided on the Knit Picks website here: http://tutorials.knitpicks.com/wptutorials/kitchener-stitch/.

Wrap and Turn (W&T)
Work until the stitch to be wrapped. If knitting: bring yarn to the front of the work, slip next st as if to purl, return the yarn to the back; turn work and slip wrapped st onto RH needle. Continue across row. If purling: bring yarn to the back of the work, slip next st as if to purl, return the yarn to the front; turn work and slip wrapped st onto RH needle. Continue across row.

Picking up wraps: Work to the wrapped st. If knitting, insert the RH needle under the wrap(s), then through the wrapped st K-wise. Knit the wrap(s) together with the wrapped st. If Purling, slip the wrapped st P-wise onto the RH needle, and use the LH needle to lift the wrap(s) and place them on the RH needle. Slip wrap(s) and unworked st back to LH needle; purl all together through the back loop.

DIRECTIONS

Cuff
Loosely CO 52 (56, 60, 64, 68) sts. PM and prepare to work in the rnd, being careful not to twist sts.
Work 2x2 Rib Pattern for 1.5." K 1 rnd. Continue to Left Leg or Right Leg.

Left Leg
K 26 (28, 30, 32, 34) sts, P 2 (3, 3, 3, 4), work Puget Sound Chart Left, P 3 (2, 3, 4, 3), work Puget Sound Chart Left, P 2 (3, 3, 3, 4), K to marker.
Continue in pattern until you have worked 10 (11, 12, 12, 13) repeats of Puget Sound Chart Left.
Continue to Heel.

Right Leg
K 13 (14, 15, 16, 17) sts, P 2 (3, 3, 3, 4), work Puget Sound Chart Right, P 3 (2, 3, 4, 3), work Puget Sound Chart Right, P 2 (3, 3, 3, 4), K to marker.
Continue in pattern until you have worked 10 (11, 12, 12, 13) repeats of Puget Sound Chart Right.
Continue to Heel.

Heel
Heel Flap
K 13 (14, 15, 16, 17) sts, turn. P 26 (28, 30, 32, 34) sts, turn. The heel is worked back and forth over only these 26 (28, 30, 32, 34) sts.
Work the following 2 rows 13 (14, 15, 16, 17) times, ending with Row 2:
Row 1 (RS): Sl 1, K to end of heel, turn.
Row 2 (WS): (Sl 1, P1) to end of heel, turn.

Turn Heel
Work the following 2 rows to set up heel turn:
Row 1 (RS): K 13 (14, 15, 16, 17), SM, K2, K2tog, K1, W&T.
Row 2 (WS): P to M, SM, P2, P2tog, P1, W&T.
Continue, working the following 2 rows 2 (2, 3, 3, 3) times, ending with Row 2.
Row 1: K to 1 before the W&T gap (SM as you pass it), K2tog, K1, W&T.
Row 2: P to 1 before the W&T gap (SM as you pass it), P2tog, P1, W&T.

Gusset
Set up gusset as follows, working in the rnd from now on:
K across the heel flap, SM as you pass it. Using the same needle, PU 13 (14, 15, 16, 17) sts along the side of the heel flap. This is Needle 1.
Work across the top of the foot, using the next 2 needles (these are Needles 2 and 3), continuing your established pattern for Puget Sound Chart Left or Puget Sound Chart Right (you will have 13 (14, 15, 16 17) sts on both Needle 2 and Needle 3).
Using your spare needle, PU 13 (14, 15, 16, 17) sts along the remaining side of the heel flap, then K to the M. This is Needle 4.
Needles 1 and 4 (sole of foot) should have 23 (25, 26, 28, 30) sts. Needles 2 and 3 (top of foot) should have 13 (14, 15, 16, 17) sts. 72 (78, 82, 88, 94) sts.

Work the following 2 rnds 10 (11, 11, 12, 13) times, ending with Rnd 2.

Rnd 1: Needle 1: K to 2 sts before end, K2tog. Needles 2 and 3: Work in pattern. Needle 4: Ssk, K to end. 2 sts dec.

Rnd 2: Needle 1: K, Needles 2 and 3: Work in pattern. Needle 4: K. 52 (56, 60, 64, 68) sts.

Foot

Work even, following established pattern until foot measures about 5.5 (6.5, 7, 7.5, 7.75)" from back of heel, or about 1.75 (2, 2.25, 2.25, 2.5)" less than desired foot length, ending on Row 6 of Puget Sound Chart Left or Puget Sound Chart Right. K 1 rnd.

Toe

Work the following rounds until 20 sts remain, ending with Rnd 2.

Rnd 1: Needle 1: K to 2 sts before end, K2tog. Needle 2: Ssk, K to end. Needle 3: K to 2 sts before end, K2tog. Needle 4: Ssk, K to end. 4 sts dec.

Rnd 2: K.

Finishing

Use the Kitchener St to close the toe.

Work second sock, being sure to end up with a matching pair (Left and Right).

Weave in any remaining ends and block.

Chart Left

4	3	2	1		
■		O	╲		6
■	╲				5
	╲	O			4
					3
			O		2
			■		1

Chart Right

4	3	2	1		
╱	O	■			6
		■	╱		5
	O	╱			4
					3
O					2
■					1

Legend

☐ **K**
Knit stitch

⊡ **P**
Purl stitch

⊙ **yo**
Yarn Over

▩ **No Stitch**

◪ **k2tog**
Knit two stitches together as one stitch

◩ **ssk**
Slip one stitch as if to knit. Slip another stitch as if to knit. Insert left-hand needle into front of these two stitches and knit them together.

SWIRL SAMPLER SOCKS

by Becky Greene

FINISHED MEASUREMENTS
7 (8, 9)" leg and foot circumference
(unstretched, blocked); foot length
is adjustable.

YARN
Knit Picks Hawthorne Tonal Hand Paint
(80% Superwash Fine Highland Wool,
20% Polyamide (Nylon); 357 yards/100g):
Springfield 27412, 1 (1, 2) skein.

NEEDLES
US 2 (2.75mm) DPNs or two 24" circular
needles for two circulars technique, or one
32" or longer circular needle for Magic
Loop technique, or size to obtain gauge

NOTIONS
Yarn Needle
Stitch Markers

GAUGE
32 sts and 40 rows = 4" in St st in the
rnd, blocked

Notes:

These socks are knit cuff down with a standard slip-stitch heel flap.

Read each chart row from right to left, as a RS rnd.

For a video demonstration of how to work the Kitchener st, see http://tutorials.knitpicks.com/wptutorials/kitchener-stitch/.

DIRECTIONS

Cuff
CO 56 (64, 72) sts. PM. Join for working in the rnd, being careful not to twist sts.

Rnds 1-15: (K2, P2) around.
Rnd 16: K.

Right Leg
Begin to work from Right charts for your size. Work Swirl 4, Swirl 3, Swirl 2, and Swirl 1 once per rnd.

Continue as established for 28 (32, 36) total rnds. On rnd 26 (30, 34), work as written until 1 st before end of rnd. Then cross the first st of the next rnd over the last unworked st of the previous row and move the first st of the Cable 2 Back to the RH needle. This will now be the last st of the rnd.

After working the first section of patterns, work one more tier as follows: Swirl 3, Swirl 2, Swirl 1, Swirl 4.
Continue as established, working all 28 (32, 36) rnds of each chart.

Heel

Turn sock, P 28 (32, 36). Turn.
Row 1 (RS): (Sl1, K1) to end.
Row 2 (WS): Sl1, P to end.
Rep Rows 1-2 14 times, or to desired heel depth.

Turn Heel

Row 1 (RS): Sl1, K14 (18, 20), SSK, K1; turn. 1 st dec.
Row 2 (WS): Sl1, P3 (P7, P7), P2tog, P1; turn. 1 st dec.
Row 3: Sl1, K to 1 st before gap, SSK, K1, turn. 1 st dec.
Row 4: Sl1, P to 1 st before gap, P2tog, P1, turn. 1 st dec.
Rep Rows 3-4 until all heel sts are worked. 16 (20, 22) sts.

Note: When working from the charts on the instep only: if the first chart begins with a YO or a SSK/K2tog dec without a matching inc/dec st, work that st as a K st. This is also true for the end of the 2nd chart for the foot. When working across instep, begin with Swirl 2 then Swirl 1. For subsequent repeats, work Swirl 1/Swirl 4, Swirl 4/Swirl 3, etc. as needed.

Gusset

Rnd 1: K across heel sts; PU 1 st in end of each row of the heel flap plus one extra in the corner before the instep; PM; K in pattern across instep; PM; PU 1 st in the corner between instep and side of heel, PU 1 st in the end of each row of the heel flap; K to first M (beginning of instep).
Rnd 2: K to M, SM, K1, SSK, K to last 3 sts before M, K2tog, K1, SM. 2 sts dec.
Rnd 3: K, slipping M.
Rep Rnds 2-3 until there are 28 (32, 36) sole sts again. 56 (64, 72) sts total.

Foot

Continue to work in pattern across instep and St st on sole until foot measures 2" short of desired foot length.

Toe

Rnd 1: *K1, SSK, K to 3 sts before M, K2tog, K1, SM; rep from *. 4 sts dec.
Rnd 2: K.
Rep Rnds 1-2 until there are 10 (12, 16) sts remaining on each of instep and sole. Use Kitchener Stitch to graft the Toe opening together.

Left Leg

Work as for right leg but use the left leg charts, working them in the order of Chart 1, Chart 2, Chart 3, Chart 4.
Note: After working Rnd 26 (30, 34), remove M for end of rnd. K1 st, PM for new start of rnd.

Finishing

Weave in ends, wash and block.

Swirl 1 Chart - Right Small

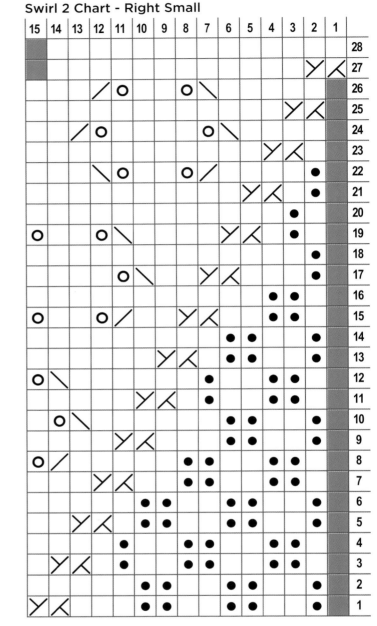

Swirl 2 Chart - Right Small

Legend

☐ **K**
Knit stitch

⬛ **P**
Purl stitch

🔘 **yo**
Yarn Over

▨ **No Stitch**

◿ **k2tog**
Knit two stitches together as one stitch

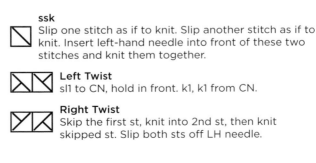

◺ **ssk**
Slip one stitch as if to knit. Slip another stitch as if to knit. Insert left-hand needle into front of these two stitches and knit them together.

Left Twist
sl1 to CN, hold in front. k1, k1 from CN.

Right Twist
Skip the first st, knit into 2nd st, then knit skipped st. Slip both sts off LH needle.

Swirl 3 Chart - Right Small

15	14	13	12	11	10	9	8	7	6	5	4	3	2	1	
▓		●	●			●	●			●	●				28
▓		●	●			●	●			●	●		⅄	⋏	27
●	●			●	●			●	●					▓	26
●	●			●	●			●	●		⅄	⋏		▓	25
		●	●			●	●			●				▓	24
		●	●			●	●			●	⅄	⋏		▓	23
●	●			●	●			●	●					▓	22
●	●			●	●			●	●	⅄	⋏			▓	21
		●	●			●	●							▓	20
		●	●			●	●		⅄	⋏				▓	19
●	●			●	●									▓	18
●	●			●	●	⅄	⋏							▓	17
		●	●			●								▓	16
		●	●			●	⅄	⋏						○	15
●	●			●	●									▓	14
●	●			●	●	⅄	⋏						○	╱	13
		●	●											▓	12
		●	●	⅄	⋏							○	╱	▓	11
●	●													▓	10
●	●	⅄	⋏						○	╱		○		▓	9
		●												▓	8
		●	⅄	⋏				○	╱		○	╱		▓	7
●	●													▓	6
●	●	⅄	⋏				○	╱		○	╱			▓	5
														▓	4
	⅄	⋏				○	╱		○	╱				▓	3
														▓	2
⅄	⋏				○	╱		○	╱					▓	1

Swirl 4 Chart - Right Small

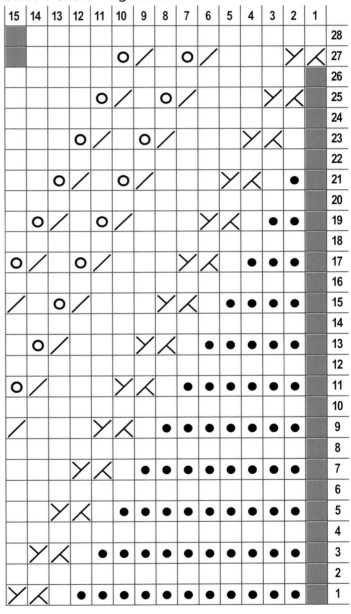

Swirl 1 Chart - Right Medium

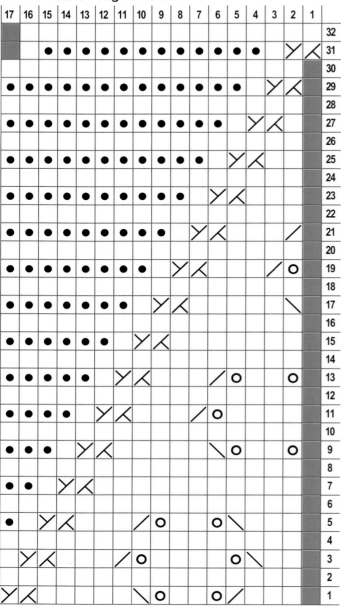

Swirl 2 Chart - Right Medium

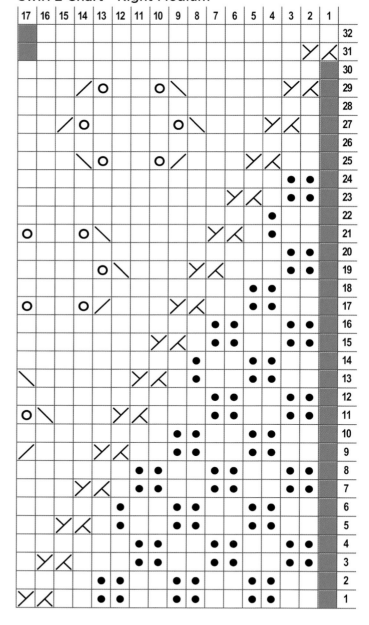

Swirl 3 Chart - Right Medium

Swirl 4 Chart - Right Medium

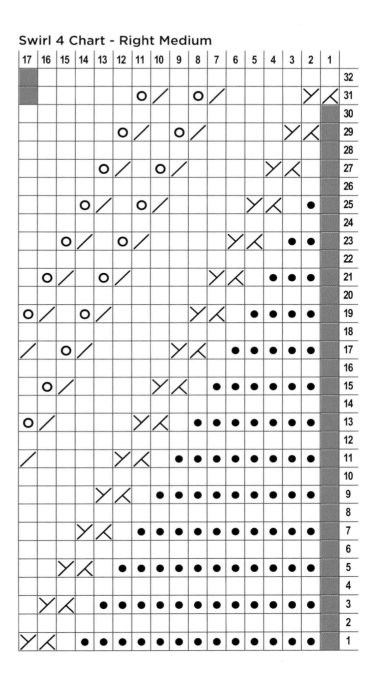

Swirl 1 Chart - Right Large

18	17	16	15	14	13	12	11	10	9	8	7	6	5	4	3	2	1	Row
▨																		36
▨		•	•	•	•	•	•	•	•	•	•	•	•	•	•	Y		35
																		34
	•	•	•	•	•	•	•	•	•	•	•	•	•	•	Y	⋏		33
																		32
•	•	•	•	•	•	•	•	•	•	•	•	•	•	Y	⋏			31
																		30
•	•	•	•	•	•	•	•	•	•	•	•	•	Y	⋏				29
																		28
•	•	•	•	•	•	•	•	•	•	•	•	Y	⋏					27
																		26
•	•	•	•	•	•	•	•	•	•	•	Y	⋏						25
																		24
•	•	•	•	•	•	•	•	•	•	Y	⋏					/		23
																		22
•	•	•	•	•	•	•	•	•	Y	⋏						/	○	21
																		20
•	•	•	•	•	•	•	•	Y	⋏								\	19
																		18
•	•	•	•	•	•	•	Y	⋏										17
																		16
•	•	•	•	•	•	Y	⋏											15
													/	○		○	\	14
•	•	•	•	•	Y	⋏												13
										/	○						○	12
•	•	•	•	Y	⋏													11
										\	○			○	/			10
•	•	•	Y	⋏														9
																		8
•	•	Y	⋏															7
																		6
•	Y	⋏						/	○			○	\					5
																		4
Y	⋏							/	○			○	\					3
																		2
Y	⋏							\	○			○	/					1

Swirl 2 Chart - Right Large

19	18	17	16	15	14	13	12	11	10	9	8	7	6	5	4	3	2	1	
▩																			36
▩																	⟩	⟨	35
																	▩		34
																⟩	⟨		33
				/	○		○	\											32
															⟩	⟨			31
				/	○			○	\								●		30
													⟩	⟨			●		29
				\	○		○	/								●			28
											⟩	⟨				●			27
																●			26
										⟩	⟨					●			25
															●	●			24
○			○	\				⟩	⟨						●	●			23
													●				●		22
				○	\		⟩	⟨					●				●		21
												●			●	●			20
○			○	/	⟩	⟨						●			●	●			19
													●	●		●			18
						⟩	⟨						●	●		●			17
											●	●			●	●			16
					⟩	⟨					●	●			●	●			15
									●	●			●	●			●		14
				⟩	⟨				●	●			●	●			●		13
								●			●	●			●	●			12
			⟩	⟨				●			●	●			●	●			11
									●	●			●	●			●		10
		⟩	⟨						●	●			●	●			●		9
							●	●			●	●			●	●			8
	⟩	⟨					●	●			●	●			●	●			7
					●	●			●	●			●	●			●		6
⟩	⟨				●	●			●	●			●	●			●		5
				●			●	●			●	●			●	●			4
⟩	⟨			●			●	●			●	●			●	●			3
					●	●		●	●		●	●	●	●			●		2
⟩	⟨				●	●		●	●		●	●	●	●			●		1

Swirl 3 Chart - Right Large

19	18	17	16	15	14	13	12	11	10	9	8	7	6	5	4	3	2	1	Row
▓		●			●	●			●	●			●	●					36
▓		●			●	●			●	●			●	●			Y	人	35
		●	●			●	●			●	●			●				▓	34
		●	●			●	●			●	●				●	Y	人	▓	33
			●	●		●	●		●	●		●						▓	32
			●	●		●	●		●	●		●			Y	人		▓	31
●			●	●			●	●			●	●						▓	30
●			●	●			●	●			●	●		Y	人			▓	29
	●	●			●	●			●	●								▓	28
	●	●			●	●			●	●		Y	人					▓	27
●			●	●			●	●			●							▓	26
●			●	●			●	●			●	Y	人					▓	25
	●	●			●	●			●									▓	24
	●	●			●	●			●		Y	人						▓	23
●			●	●			●	●										▓	22
●			●	●			●	●	Y	人								▓	21
	●	●			●	●												▓	20
	●	●			●	●	Y	人									O	▓	19
●			●	●		●												▓	18
●			●	●		●	Y	人								O	/	▓	17
	●	●		●														▓	16
	●	●		●	Y	人									O	/		▓	15
●			●	●														▓	14
●			●	●	Y	人					O	/		O				▓	13
	●	●																▓	12
	●	●	Y	人					O	/		O	/					▓	11
●			●															▓	10
●			●	Y	人		O	/		O	/							▓	9
	●																	▓	8
	●	Y	人		O	/		O	/									▓	7
●																		▓	6
●	Y	人		O	/		O	/										▓	5
																		▓	4
Y	人		O	/		O	/											▓	3
																		▓	2
Y	人	O	/		O	/												▓	1

Swirl 4 Chart - Right Large

19	18	17	16	15	14	13	12	11	10	9	8	7	6	5	4	3	2	1	
																			36
							O	/		O	/						Y	⋏	35
																			34
						O	/		O	/						Y	⋏		33
																			32
					O	/		O	/						Y	⋏			31
																			30
				O	/		O	/						Y	⋏		●		29
																			28
			O	/		O	/						Y	⋏		●	●		27
																			26
		O	/		O	/						Y	⋏		●	●	●		25
																			24
	O	/		O	/						Y	⋏		●	●	●	●		23
																			22
O	/		O	/						Y	⋏		●	●	●	●	●		21
																			20
/		O	/						Y	⋏		●	●	●	●	●	●		19
																			18
	O	/						Y	⋏		●	●	●	●	●	●	●		17
																			16
O	/						Y	⋏		●	●	●	●	●	●	●	●		15
																			14
/						Y	⋏		●	●	●	●	●	●	●	●	●		13
																			12
					Y	⋏		●	●	●	●	●	●	●	●	●	●		11
																			10
				Y	⋏		●	●	●	●	●	●	●	●	●	●	●		9
																			8
			Y	⋏		●	●	●	●	●	●	●	●	●	●	●	●		7
																			6
		Y	⋏		●	●	●	●	●	●	●	●	●	●	●	●	●		5
																			4
	Y	⋏		●	●	●	●	●	●	●	●	●	●	●	●	●	●		3
																			2
Y	⋏		●	●	●	●	●	●	●	●	●	●	●	●	●	●	●		1

Swirl 1 Chart - Left Small

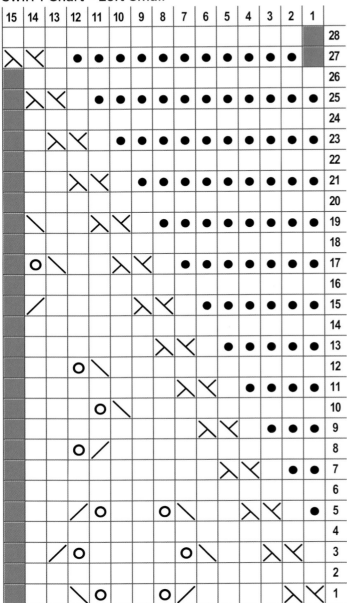

Swirl 2 Chart - Left Small

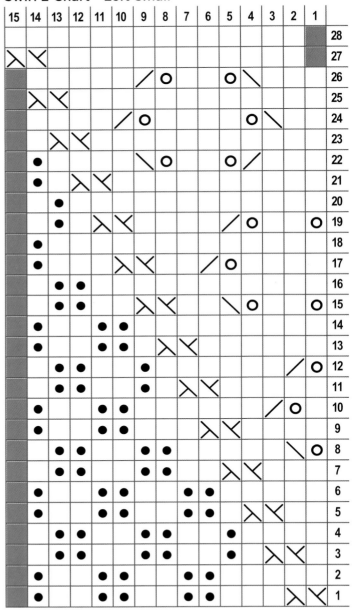

Swirl 3 Chart - Left Small

15	14	13	12	11	10	9	8	7	6	5	4	3	2	1	
				●	●			●	●			●	●	▓	28
⟋	⟍			●	●			●	●			●	●	▓	27
▓			●			●	●			●	●			●	26
▓	⟋	⟍	●			●	●			●	●			●	25
▓				●	●			●	●			●	●		24
▓		⟋	⟍	●	●			●	●			●	●		23
▓						●	●			●	●			●	22
▓			⟋	⟍		●	●			●	●			●	21
▓								●	●			●	●		20
▓				⟋	⟍			●	●			●	●		19
▓							●			●	●			●	18
▓					⟋	⟍	●			●	●			●	17
▓								●	●			●	●		16
▓	O				⟋	⟍		●	●			●	●		15
▓										●	●			●	14
▓	\	O					⟋	⟍		●	●			●	13
▓												●	●		12
▓		\	O					⟋	⟍			●	●		11
▓										●				●	10
▓	O		\	O				⟋	⟍	●				●	9
▓												●	●		8
▓	\	O		\	O			⟋	⟍			●	●		7
▓														●	6
▓	\	O		\	O				⟋	⟍				●	5
▓															4
▓		\	O		\	O				⟋	⟍				3
▓															2
▓			\	O		\	O					⟋	⟍		1

Swirl 4 Chart - Left Small

15	14	13	12	11	10	9	8	7	6	5	4	3	2	1	
														▓	28
⟋	⟍					\	O		\	O				▓	27
▓															26
▓	⟋	⟍					\	O		\	O				25
▓															24
▓		⟋	⟍					\	O		\	O			23
▓															22
▓	●		⟋	⟍					\	O		\	O		21
▓															20
▓	●	●		⟋	⟍					\	O		\	O	19
▓															18
▓	●	●	●		⟋	⟍					\	O		O	17
▓															16
▓	●	●	●	●		⟋	⟍					\	O	\	15
▓															14
▓	●	●	●	●	●		⟋	⟍					\	O	13
▓															12
▓	●	●	●	●	●	●		⟋	⟍				\	O	11
▓															10
▓	●	●	●	●	●	●	●		⟋	⟍				\	9
▓															8
▓	●	●	●	●	●	●	●	●		⟋	⟍			\	7
▓															6
▓	●	●	●	●	●	●	●	●	●		⟋	⟍			5
▓															4
▓	●	●	●	●	●	●	●	●	●	●		⟋	⟍		3
▓															2
▓	●	●	●	●	●	●	●	●	●	●	●		⟋	⟍	1

Swirl 1 Chart - Left Medium

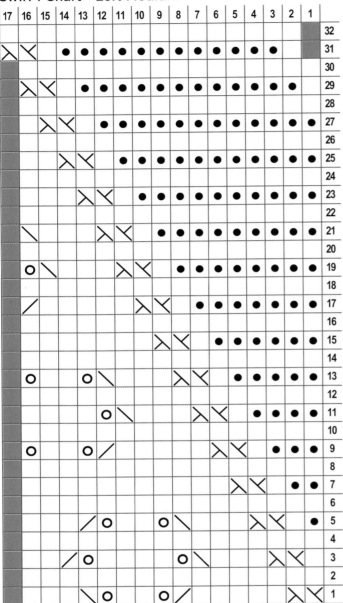

Swirl 2 Chart - Left Medium

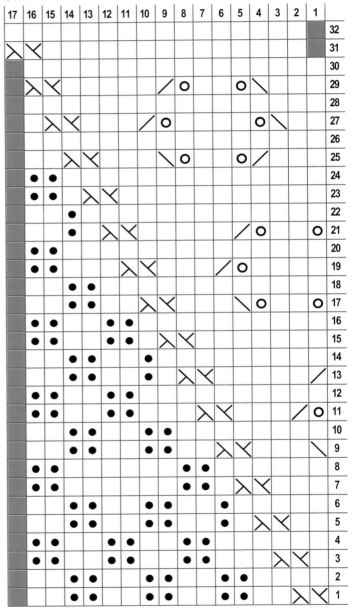

Swirl 3 Chart - Left Medium

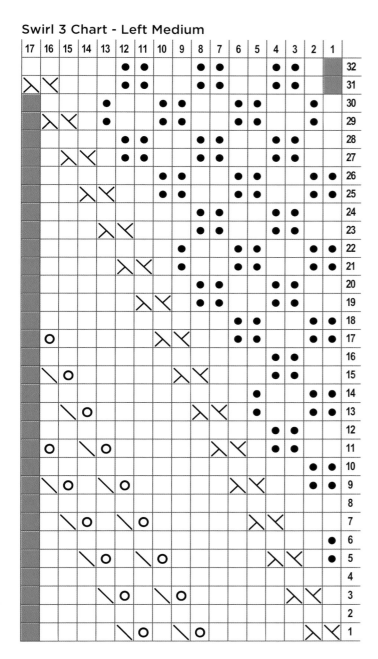

Swirl 4 Chart - Left Medium

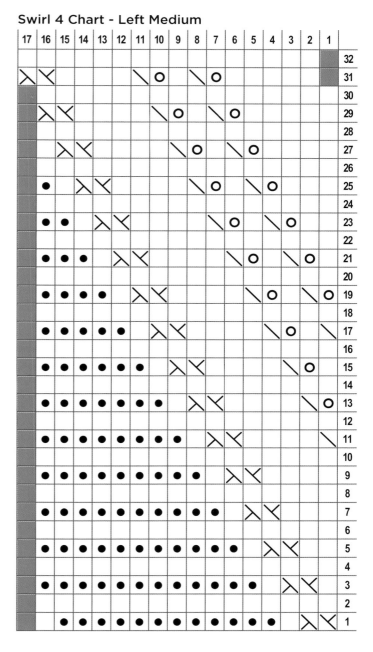

Swirl 1 Chart - Left Large

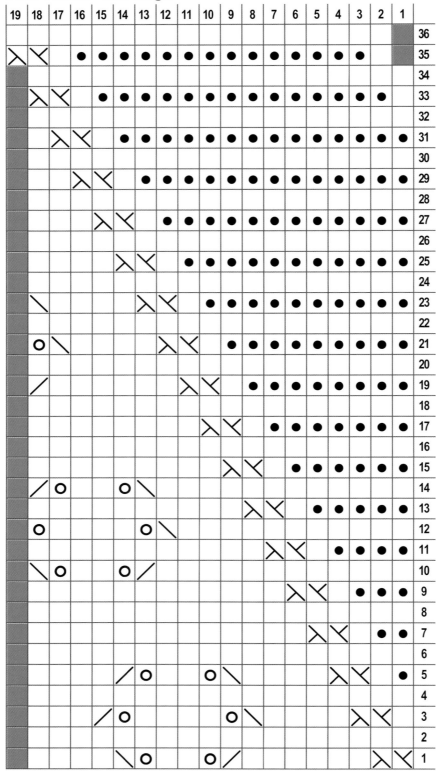

Swirl 2 Chart - Left Large

19	18	17	16	15	14	13	12	11	10	9	8	7	6	5	4	3	2	1	
																		▩	36
⋋	⋌																	▩	35
▩																			34
▩	⋋	⋌																	33
▩										/	○			○	\				32
▩		⋋	⋌																31
▩	●								/	○				○	\				30
▩	●		⋋	⋌															29
▩		●							\	○				○	/				28
▩		●		⋋	⋌														27
▩	●																		26
▩	●				⋋	⋌													25
▩		●	●																24
▩		●	●			⋋	⋌						/	○				○	23
▩	●			●															22
▩	●			●			⋋	⋌				/	○						21
▩		●	●			●													20
▩		●	●			●		⋋	⋌				\	○				○	19
▩	●			●	●														18
▩	●			●	●				⋋	⋌									17
▩		●	●			●	●												16
▩		●	●			●	●			⋋	⋌								15
▩	●			●	●			●	●										14
▩	●			●	●			●	●	⋋	⋌								13
▩		●	●			●	●			●								/	12
▩		●	●			●	●			●	⋋	⋌							11
▩	●			●	●			●	●										10
▩	●			●	●			●	●	⋋	⋌								9
▩		●	●			●	●			●	●								8
▩		●	●			●	●			●	●	⋋	⋌						7
▩	●			●	●			●	●			●	●						6
▩	●			●	●			●	●			●	●	⋋	⋌				5
▩		●	●			●	●			●	●			●					4
▩		●	●			●	●			●	●			●	⋋	⋌			3
▩	●			●	●			●	●			●	●						2
▩	●			●	●			●	●			●	●			⋋	⋌		1

Swirl 3 Chart - Left Large

19	18	17	16	15	14	13	12	11	10	9	8	7	6	5	4	3	2	1	
				●	●			●	●			●	●			●		▨	36
⟋	⟍			●	●			●	●			●	●			●		▨	35
▨			●			●	●			●	●			●	●				34
▨	⟋	⟍		●		●	●			●	●			●	●				33
▨					●	●	●			●	●					●	●		32
▨		⟋	⟍		●			●	●		●	●				●	●		31
▨						●	●			●	●			●	●			●	30
▨			⟋	⟍		●	●			●	●			●	●			●	29
▨								●	●			●	●			●	●		28
▨				⟋	⟍			●	●			●	●			●	●		27
▨							●			●	●			●	●			●	26
▨					⟋	⟍	●			●	●			●	●			●	25
▨									●			●	●			●	●		24
▨						⟋	⟍		●			●	●			●	●		23
▨										●	●			●	●			●	22
▨							⟋	⟍		●	●			●	●			●	21
▨												●	●			●	●		20
▨	○							⟋	⟍			●	●			●	●		19
▨											●			●	●			●	18
▨	╲	○							⟋	⟍	●			●	●			●	17
▨														●	●	●	●		16
▨		╲	○							⟋	⟍		●			●	●		15
▨														●	●			●	14
▨	○		╲	○							⟋	⟍		●	●			●	13
▨																●	●		12
▨	╲	○		╲	○							⟋	⟍			●	●		11
▨															●			●	10
▨		╲	○		╲	○							⟋	⟍	●			●	9
▨																●			8
▨			╲	○		╲	○							⟋	⟍	●			7
▨																		●	6
▨				╲	○		╲	○							⟋	⟍		●	5
▨																			4
▨					╲	○		╲	○							⟋	⟍		3
▨																			2
▨				╲	○		╲	○								⟋	⟍		1

Swirl 4 Chart - Left Large

19	18	17	16	15	14	13	12	11	10	9	8	7	6	5	4	3	2	1	
																		▨	36
⋋	⋌						\	O		\	O							▨	35
▨																			34
▨	⋋	⋌						\	O		\	O							33
▨																			32
▨		⋋	⋌						\	O		\	O						31
▨																			30
▨	●		⋋	⋌						\	O		\	O					29
▨																			28
▨	●	●		⋋	⋌						\	O		\	O				27
▨																			26
▨	●	●	●		⋋	⋌						\	O		\	O			25
▨																			24
▨	●	●	●	●		⋋	⋌						\	O		\	O		23
▨																			22
▨	●	●	●	●	●		⋋	⋌						\	O		\	O	21
▨																			20
▨	●	●	●	●	●	●		⋋	⋌						\	O		\	19
▨																			18
▨	●	●	●	●	●	●	●		⋋	⋌						\	O		17
▨																			16
▨	●	●	●	●	●	●	●	●		⋋	⋌						\	O	15
▨																			14
▨	●	●	●	●	●	●	●	●	●		⋋	⋌						\	13
▨																			12
▨	●	●	●	●	●	●	●	●	●	●		⋋	⋌						11
▨																			10
▨	●	●	●	●	●	●	●	●	●	●	●		⋋	⋌					9
▨																			8
▨	●	●	●	●	●	●	●	●	●	●	●	●		⋋	⋌				7
▨																			6
▨	●	●	●	●	●	●	●	●	●	●	●	●	●		⋋	⋌			5
▨																			4
▨	●	●	●	●	●	●	●	●	●	●	●	●	●	●		⋋	⋌		3
▨																			2
▨	●	●	●	●	●	●	●	●	●	●	●	●	●	●	●		⋋	⋌	1

TEXTURED LACE SOCKS

by Lori Wagner

FINISHED MEASUREMENTS

7.5 (8, 8.5)" finished foot circumference; socks meant to be worn with 1" negative ease.

YARN

Knit Picks Hawthorne Multi

Yarn (80% Superwash Fine Highland Wool, 20% Polyamide (Nylon); 357 yards/100g): Kerns 27423, 2 skeins.

NEEDLES

US 1 (2.25mm) DPNs or two 24" circular needles for two circulars technique, or one 32" or longer circular needle for Magic Loop technique, or size to obtain gauge.

NOTIONS

Yarn Needle
Removable Stitch Marker

GAUGE

36 sts and 48 rows = 4" in St st in the rnd, blocked.
32 sts and 56 rows = 4" over Chart B in the rnd, blocked.

Resembling the twists and turns of rocky hiking trails and flowing streams, the Textured Lace socks have the look of cables but actually use an addicting textured lace pattern!

The top-down Textured Lace socks begins with a twisted rib pattern that flows into the textured lace that is worked around the length of the leg. The stitches are then divided and a slipped stitch heel is worked. The textured lace pattern continues through the instep with a stockinette stitch sole. The decrease for the toe continues in stockinette stitch with the remaining stitches grafted to close the opening at the end.

The charts are worked in the rnd. Read each row from right to left as a RS row.

Picking Up Stitches

When picking up sts along the heel flap, insert needle tip under both legs of the slipped st along the edge of the heel flap, wrap the yarn around your needle K-wise and pull through onto RH needle. Continue this along the edge of the heel flap.

DIRECTIONS

Cuff

CO 64 (68, 72) sts with a Long Tail CO or elastic CO of your choice, and join for working in the rnd, distributing sts on needles as you prefer and being careful not to twist the sts. Mark the beginning of the rnd with a removable marker.

Size 7.5 Only, Rnds 1-12: *K1 TBL, P1, K2 TBL, (P1, K1 TBL) 4 times, P1, K2 TBL, P2, K2 TBL, (P1, K1 TBL) 4 times, P1, K2 TBL, P1, K1 TBL; rep from * around.

Size 8 Only, Rnds 1-12: *K1 TBL, P1, K2 TBL, (P1, K1 TBL) 4 times, (P1, K2 TBL) three times, (P1, K1 TBL) 4 times, P1, K2 TBL, P1, K1 TBL; rep from * around.

Size 8.5 Only, Rnds 1-12: *K1 TBL, P2, K2 TBL, (P1, K1 TBL) 4 times, (P1, K2 TBL) three times, (P1, K1 TBL) 4 times, P1, K2 TBL, P2, K1 TBL; rep from * around.

Both Socks Leg

Knit 1 rnd.
Work Rnds 1-12 of Chart A for the size you are making 7 times. Each chart row will be repeated twice around.

Heel

Right Heel
Set-up Row 1 (RS): K32 (34, 36), turn work.
Set-up Row 2 (WS): P32 (34, 36), turn work.
Heel flap is worked over these 32 (34, 36) sts. Rearrange sts as you prefer on needles. Remaining 32 (34, 36) sts will be worked later for instep.

Left Heel
Set-up Row 1 (RS): Work Row 1 of Chart A for size you are making once, K32 (34, 36), turn work.
Set-up Row 2 (WS): P32 (34, 36), turn work.
Heel flap is worked over these 32 (34, 36) sts. Rearrange sts as you prefer on needles. Remaining 32 (34, 36) sts will be worked later for instep.

Both Socks Heel
Work heel sts back and forth in rows as follows:
Row 1 (RS): *Sl1 P-wise WYIB, K1; rep from * across.
Row 2 (WS): *Sl 1 P-wise WYIB, P across.
Rep these 2 rows 15 (16, 17) times more. 32 (34, 36) rows total, 16 (17, 18) slipped selvedge sts.

Turn Heel
Work short rows to shape heel as follows:
Row 1 (RS): K18 (19, 20), SSK, K1, turn work. 1 st dec.
Row 2 (WS): Sl1 P-wise WYIB, P5, P2tog, P1, turn work. 1 st dec.
Row 3: Sl1 P-wise WYIB, K to 1 st before gap, SSK (1 st from each side of gap), K1, turn work. 1 st dec.
Row 4: Sl 1 P-wise, P to 1 st before gap, P2tog (1 st from each side of gap), P1, turn work. 1 st dec.
Rep Rows 3 and 4 four (four, five) times more.

Final Row 1 (RS): K to 1 st before gap, SSK (1 st from each side of gap), K0 (1, 0). 1 st dec.
Final Row 2 (WS): P to 1 st before gap, P2tog (1 st from each side of gap), P0 (1, 0). 1 st dec.

Shape Gussets

Right Gusset Set-up

PU sts along selvedge edges of heel flap and rejoin for working in the rnd as follows:

Set up Gusset: K18 (20, 20) heel sts, PU and K16 (17, 18) sts along the first edge of heel flap (see Notes regarding Picking Up Stitches), work Row 1 of Chart A once for instep sts, PU and K16 (17, 18) sts along the second edge of the heel flap, K9 (10, 10) to center of heel. 82 (88, 92) sts.
This is the new start of rnd; rearrange sts or place removable marker as you prefer.

Left Gusset Set-Up

PU sts along selvedge edges of heel flap and rejoin for working in the rnd as follows:

Set up Gusset: K18 (20, 20) heel sts, PU and K16 (17, 18) sts along the first edge of heel flap (see Notes regarding Picking Up Stitches), work Row 2 of Chart A once for instep sts, PU and K16 (17, 18) sts along the second edge of the heel flap, K9 (10, 10) to center of heel. 82 (88, 92) sts.
This is the new start of rnd; rearrange sts or place removable marker as you prefer.

Gusset Both Socks

Gusset Rnd 1: K to 3 sts before instep, K2tog, K1, work Chart A in pattern once across instep sts, K1, SSK, K to end of rnd. 2 sts dec.
Gusset Rnd 2: K to instep, work Chart A in pattern once across instep sts, K to end of rnd.
Rep Gusset Rnds 1 – 2 keeping in pattern eight (nine, nine) more times. 64 (68, 72) sts.

Foot

Work rnds keeping instep in pattern and remainder in St st until sock measures, from back of heel, 3" less than desired foot total length and completing a full repeat of stitch pattern of Chart A.

Work Rnds 1 – 12 once for instep sts from Chart B for the size you are making.

Knit around until sock measures, from back of heel, 2" less than desired total foot length.

Toe

Set-Up: Remove end of rnd marker, K16 (17, 18) to end of sole.
This is the new start of rnd at the beginning of the instep; rearrange sts or place a removable marker as you prefer. The first half of the sts are the instep, the second half are the sole.

Rnd 1: K1, SSK, K to 3 sts before end of instep, K2tog, K2, SSK, K to 3 sts before end of sole, K2tog, K1. 4 sts dec.
Rnd 2: Knit.
Work Rnds 1 and 2 seven (seven, eight) more times. 32 (36, 36) sts.
Work Rnd 1 only 5 (6, 6) times. 12 sts.

Finishing

Cut yarn, leaving a 12" tail, graft remaining sts. Weave in loose ends and block to measurements.

Chart A (Small Size)

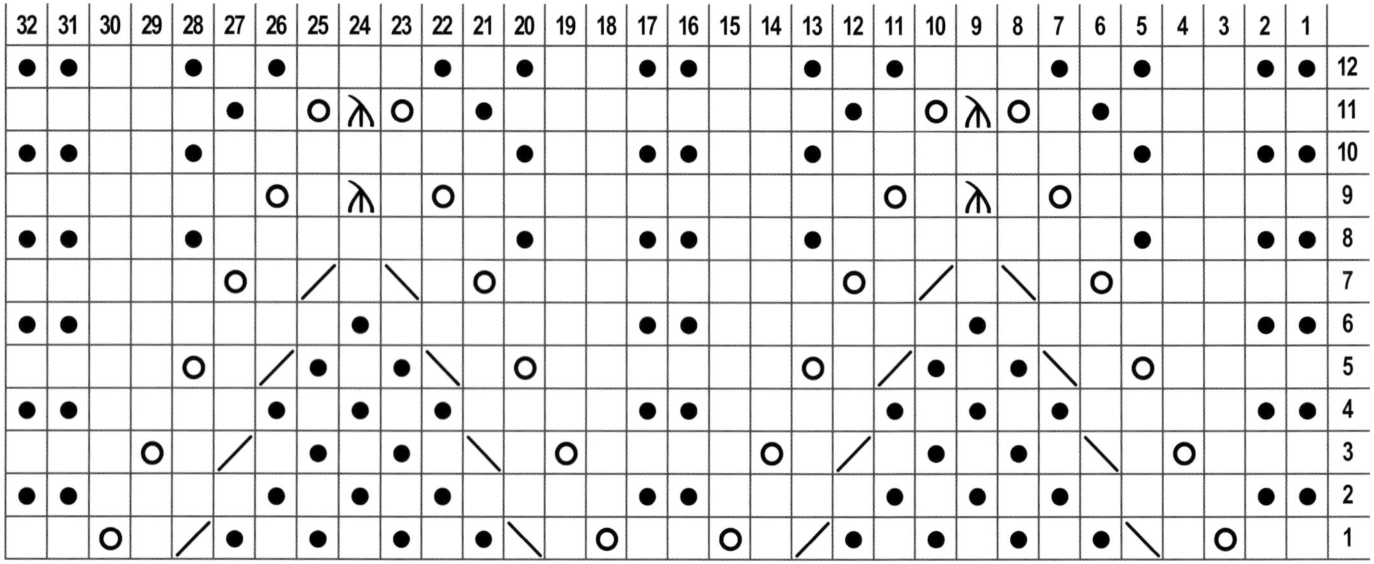

A 32-column by 12-row knitting chart. Columns are numbered 1–32 left to right across the top; rows are numbered 12 (top) down to 1 (bottom) along the right side. Cells contain the following symbols: knit (blank box), purl (●), yarn over (O), k2tog (╱), ssk (╲), and sl1 k2tog psso (special symbol).

Legend

K
Knit stitch — □

P
Purl stitch — ●

yo
Yarn Over — O

k2tog
Knit two stitches together as one stitch — ╱

ssk
Slip one stitch as if to knit. Slip another stitch as if to knit. Insert left-hand needle into front of these two stitches and knit them together. — ╲

sl1 k2tog psso
slip 1, k2tog, pass slip stitch over. — ⋀

Chart A (Medium Size)

Round	12	11	10	9	8	7	6	5	4	3	2	1
1	●		●		●		●		●		●	
2	●		●		●		●		●		●	
3												O
4										O		
5	●		●		●			O				/
6		●				O				/		●
7	●			O				/				
8						O		/		●		●
9		⋏		⋏			●		●		●	
10				O			/		●		●	
11	●			O			/		●		●	
12		●				O		/				●
13	●		●		●			O				/
14										O		
15												O
16	●		●		●		●		●		●	
17	●		●		●		●		●		●	
18	●		●		●		●		●		●	
19	●		●		●		●		●		●	
20												O
21										O		
22	●		●		●			O				/
23		●				O				/		●
24	●			O				/				
25						O		/		●		●
26		⋏		⋏			●		●		●	
27				O			/		●		●	
28	●			O			/		●		●	
29		●				O		/				●
30	●		●		●			O				/
31										O		
32												O
33	●		●		●		●		●		●	
34	●		●		●		●		●		●	

Chart A (Large Size)

Round	12	11	10	9	8	7	6	5	4	3	2	1
1	●		●		●		●		●		●	
2	●		●		●		●		●		●	
3	●		●		●		●		●		●	
4												O
5										O		
6	●		●		●			O				/
7		●				O				/		●
8	●			O				/				
9						O		/		●		●
10		⋏		⋏			●		●		●	
11				O			/		●		●	
12	●			O			/		●		●	
13		●				O		/				●
14	●		●		●			O				/
15										O		
16												O
17	●		●		●		●		●		●	
18	●		●		●		●		●		●	
19	●		●		●		●		●		●	
20	●		●		●		●		●		●	
21												O
22										O		
23	●		●		●			O				/
24		●				O				/		●
25	●			O				/				
26						O		/		●		●
27		⋏		⋏			●		●		●	
28				O			/		●		●	
29	●			O			/		●		●	
30		●				O		/				●
31	●		●		●			O				/
32										O		
33												O
34	●		●		●		●		●		●	
35	●		●		●		●		●		●	
36	●		●		●		●		●		●	

Chart B (Small Size)

Row	12	11	10	9	8	7	6	5	4	3	2	1
1	●		●		●		●		●		●	
2	●		●		●		●		●		●	
3												O
4										O		
5								O				/
6						O			/			●
7				O			/		●		●	
8		O				/	●		●		●	
9		⋏		⋏				●				
10		O				\	●		●		●	
11				O			\	●				
12						O			\			●
13								O				\
14										O		
15												O
16	●		●		●		●		●		●	
17	●		●		●		●		●		●	
18												O
19										O		
20								O				/
21						O			/			●
22				O			/		●		●	
23		O				/	●		●		●	
24		⋏		⋏				●				
25		O				\	●		●		●	
26				O			\	●				
27						O			\			●
28								O				\
29										O		
30												O
31	●		●		●		●		●		●	
32	●		●		●		●		●		●	

Chart B (Medium Size)

Row	12	11	10	9	8	7	6	5	4	3	2	1
1	●		●		●		●		●		●	
2	●		●		●		●		●		●	
3												O
4										O		
5								O				/
6						O			/			●
7				O			/		●		●	
8		O				/	●		●		●	
9		⋏		⋏				●				
10		O				\	●		●		●	
11				O			\	●				
12						O			\			●
13								O				\
14										O		
15												O
16	●		●		●		●		●		●	
17	●		●		●		●		●		●	
18	●		●		●		●		●		●	
19	●		●		●		●		●		●	
20												O
21										O		
22								O				/
23						O			/			●
24				O			/		●		●	
25		O				/	●		●		●	
26		⋏		⋏				●				
27		O				\	●		●		●	
28				O			\	●				
29						O			\			●
30								O				\
31										O		
32												O
33	●		●		●		●		●		●	
34	●		●		●		●		●		●	

Chart B (Large Size)

Row	12	11	10	9	8	7	6	5	4	3	2	1
1	●		●		●		●		●		●	
2	●		●		●		●		●		●	
3	●		●		●		●		●		●	
4												○
5										○		
6								○				/
7						○				/		●
8				○				/	●		●	
9		○				/			●		●	
10		⅄		⅄			●		●		●	
11		○				\	●		●		●	
12				○				\	●		●	
13						○				\		●
14								○				\
15										○		
16												○
17	●		●		●		●		●		●	
18	●		●		●		●		●		●	
19	●		●		●		●		●		●	
20	●		●		●		●		●		●	
21												○
22										○		
23								○				/
24						○				/		●
25				○				/	●		●	
26		○				/			●		●	
27		⅄		⅄			●		●		●	
28		○				\	●		●		●	
29				○				\	●		●	
30						○				\		●
31								○				\
32										○		
33												○
34	●		●		●		●		●		●	
35	●		●		●		●		●		●	
36	●		●		●		●		●		●	

TIME LORD SOCKS

by Margaret Mills

FINISHED MEASUREMENTS

7.75 (8.75, 9.75)" leg and foot circumference.

YARN

Knit Picks Stroll Sock Yarn

(75% Superwash Merino Wool, 25% Nylon; 231 yards/50g): Sapphire Heather 24590, 2 balls.

NEEDLES

US 2 (2.75mm) DPNs or two 24" circular needles for two circulars technique, or one 32" or longer circular needle for Magic Loop technique, or size to obtain gauge.

NOTIONS

Yarn Needle
Stitch Markers (6)
Cable Needle
Scrap Yarn or Stitch Holder

GAUGE

32 sts and 48 rows = 4" in St st in the rnd, blocked.
28 sts = 2.5" over Chart 1 in the rnd, unstretched.

For pattern support, contact
margaretgracemills@gmail.com

Notes:

Triple-stranded DNA occurs in certain circumstances in nature, as a structure that can be transitory or stable. For example, the gene editing technology CRISPR involves a "guide" RNA strand binding to a homologous stretch of double-stranded DNA and thereby directing a nuclease to cut the DNA at a particular spot along that stretch.

But in science fiction, triple-helical DNA is the structure for many alien genomes, most notably the Time Lords in Doctor Who. That's right: Doctor Who DNA socks.

These socks feature triple-stranded helices twisting down each side of the leg while a single strand wanders down the front. The triple helices denature (open up and separate their strands) at the ankle: one strand travels down the heel flap, one travels down each side of the foot, and the third strand from each helix annealing (joining together) with the solo strand from the leg to form a new triple helix twisting down the center of the foot.

The socks are knit top-down, with a very large chart for the rearranging of DNA strands and a somewhat tricky heel flap (requiring cabling on right and wrong side rows, and following different chart rows on the two sides of the flap).

Note on Gauge:

The width of the socks is dependent on your gauge over the cable pattern as well as your gauge in Stockinette stitch. Knit a swatch in the round and test gauge in both Stockinette stitch and Chart 1.

There are 6 versions of Chart 3, two for each size, one each for Right and Left socks. When working charts in the rnd read each row from right to left. When working charts flat, read RS rows from right to left and WS rows from left to right.

1x1 Twisted Rib (worked in the rnd over an even number of sts)
All Rnds: (K1TBL, P1) to end.

M1p (Make 1 P-wise): PU the strand between the st just worked and the first st on the left needle. P1TBL. 1 st made.
M1k (Make 1 K-wise): PU the strand between the st just worked and the first st on the left needle and K into it. 1 st made.

DIRECTIONS

Left Sock

Cuff

CO 68 (76, 84) sts. Join and work in the round, being careful not to twist.
Work in 1x1 Twisted Rib for 12 rnds.

Setup Rnd: PM(1), K1TBL, P1, K1TBL, K3, C2Fk, K2, K1TBL, M1p, P1, K1TBL, PM(2), K6 (8, 10), PM(3), K9, K1TBL, PM(4), M1k, K5 (7, 9), PM(5), K1TBL, P1, M1p, K1TBL, K2, C2Bk, K3, K1TBL, P1, K1TBL, PM(6), K21 (25, 29). 71 (79, 87) sts.

Leg

Follow Row 16 of Chart 1 between Markers 1 and 2 ("band A"), K6 (8, 10), follow Row 1 (1, 28) of Chart 2 between Markers 3 and 4 ("front strand"), K6 (8, 10), follow Row 1 of Chart 1 between Markers 5 and 6 ("band B"), K21 (25, 29).

Work from Charts 1 and 2 between Markers as established, working: Rows 17-30 then Rows 1-28 of Chart 1 on band A; Rows 2-30 then Rows 1-13 (Size 9.75" only: Rows 29-30 then Rows 1-30 then Rows 1-10) of Chart 2 on the front strand; and Rows 2-30 then rows 1-13 of Chart 1 on band B, ending 4 sts before the end of the rnd. Move Marker 1 to this spot: this is the new start of rnd.

Denaturing the Helices

Find the Left sock version of Chart 3 appropriate for your size.
Next Rnd: Work Row 1 of Chart 3-Left across the next 58 (62, 66) sts, removing Markers 2 through 5 as you encounter them, and moving Marker 6 4 sts to the end of Chart 3. K13 (17, 21).
Continue to follow Chart 3-Left as established between the markers, through Row 17 (17, 20).

Heel Flap

Starting at Marker 1, follow Row 21 (21, 25) of Chart 4 across the next 10 sts as follows: K1TBL, P4, K2, Sl1, K1, Sl1. K1. Turn.
Next Row (WS): Sl1, follow Row 22 (22, 26) of Chart 4 to Marker 1 as established, P13 (17, 21) to Marker 6, work Row 1 (1, 5) of Chart 4 across the next 10 sts as follows: P1TBL, K4, P5. P1. Turn. Put remaining sts on a holder and work these 35 (39, 43) sts back and forth for the heel flap.

Note: The two bands running down either side of the heel flap are slightly out-of-sync, and you have to keep track of the appropriate row for each DNA strand separately. This difference will be evened up when the heel is turned.

Next Row (RS): Sl1, follow Row 2 (2, 6) of Chart 4 across the next 10 sts as follows: K1, Sl1, K1, K5, K1TBL. K1, [Sl1, K1] 6x (8x, 10x), follow Row 23 (23, 27) of Chart 4 as established, K1.
Continue the heel flap as established, slipping first st of every row, working Chart 4 across the two bands as appropriate (and repeating rows 1-40 as necessary) and working the slip-stitch pattern as established in the panel between the bands, until the heel flap measures 2.5", ending with a WS row.

Turn Heel

Sl1, work appropriate row of Chart, remove Marker 6, K11 (13, 15), SSK, K1, turn. 1 st dec.
Next Row (WS): Sl1, P10, P2tog, P1, turn. 1 st dec.
Next Row (RS): Sl1, K11, SSK, K1, turn. 1 st dec.
Next Row: Sl1, P12, P2tog, P1, turn. 1 st dec.
Next Row: Sl1, K13, SSK, K1, turn. 1 st dec.
Continue in this manner, working one additional st each row, until all heel flap sts are incorporated, ending with a WS row. (Remove Marker 1 when you reach it.) Turn. 23 (25, 27) sts.

Gusset

K across 23 (25, 27) heel sts, then PU and K one st for each slipped st along the side of the heel flap. PM(1). Work across instep as follows: work Row 28 (1, 1) of Chart 2 across the first 10 sts (band A), PM(2), K1 (3, 5), PM(3), work Row 1 of Chart 1 across the next 14 sts (front strand), PM(4), K1 (3, 5), PM(5), work Row 13 (16, 16) of Chart 2 across the final 10 sts (band B), PM(6). PU and K one st for each slipped st along the next edge of the heel flap.
Next Rnd: K across heel sts, then KTBL sts along the side of the heel flap (gusset sts) until 2 gusset sts remain, K2tog SM(1). Work across instep as follows: work Row 29 (29, 2) of Chart 2 across band A, SM(2), K 1 (3, 5), SM(3), work Row 2 of Chart 1 across the front strand, SM(4), K1 (3, 5), SM(5), work Row 14 (14, 17) of Chart 2 across band B. SM(6), SSK first 2 gusset sts, KTBL remaining gusset sts.
Next Rnd: K across heel and gusset sts, work across instep as established, K across gusset sts.
Next Rnd: K across heel sts, K to final 2 gusset sts, K2tog, work across instep as established, SSK first 2 gusset sts, K remaining gusset sts. 2 sts dec.
Rep these last 2 rnds until 71 (79, 87) sts remain: 36 (40, 44) sts across instep and 35 (39, 43) sts in gusset and heel sts combined.

Foot

Work all sts as established until foot measures 1.75 (2, 2.25)" less from back of heel than total length desired. Start of rnd is now located at mid-point of sole sts. Note that there are an odd number of sole sts; where exactly you put the new start of rnd isn't important as long as it's somewhere near the middle st.

Toe Decreases

Setup Rnd: K sole sts, SM(1), work the appropriate row of Chart 2 across band A, remove Marker 2, K1 (3, 5), remove Marker 3, work the appropriate row of Chart 1 across the front strand and dec one st in the strand, remove Marker 4, K1 (3, 5), remove Marker 5, work the appropriate row of Chart 2 across band B, SM6, K sole sts. 70 (78, 86) sts.
Next Rnd: *K to 3 sts before M, K2tog, K1, SM, K1, SSK, rep from * once more, K to end of rnd. 4 sts dec.
Next Rnd: K.
Rep these last 2 rnds until 26 (26, 30) sts remain, ending with a dec rnd. K across remaining sole sts. Break yarn. Use Kitchener stitch to graft toe closed.

Right Sock

Cuff

CO 68 (76, 84) sts. Join and work in the rnd, being careful not to twist.

Work in 1x1 Twisted Rib for 12 rnds.

Setup Rnd: PM(1), K1TBL, P1, K1TBL, K3, C2Fk, K2, K1TBL, M1p, P1, K1TBL, PM(2), K5 (7, 9), M1k, PM(3), K1TBL, K9, PM(4), K6 (8, 10), PM(5), K1TBL, P1, M1p, K1TBL, K2, C2Bk, K3, K1TBL, P1, K1TBL, PM(6), K21 (25, 29). 71 (79, 87) sts.

Leg

Follow Row 16 of Chart 1 between Markers 1 and 2 ("band A"), K6 (8, 10), follow Row 16 (16, 13) of Chart 2 between Markers 3 and 4 ("front strand"), K6 (8, 10), follow Row 1 of Chart 1 between Markers 5 and 6 ("band B"), K21 (25, 29).

Work from Charts 1 and 2 between Markers as established, working: Rows 17-30 then Rows 1-28 of Chart 1 on band A; Rows 17-30 then Rows 1-28 (Size 9.75" only: Rows 14-30 then Rows 1-25) of Chart 2 on the front strand; and Rows 2-30 then Rows 1-13 of Chart 1 on band B, ending 4 sts before the end of the rnd. Move Marker 1 to this spot: this is the new start of rnd.

Denaturing the Helices

Find the Right sock version of Chart 3 appropriate for your size.

Next Rnd: Work Row 1 of Chart 3-Right across the next 58 (62, 66) sts, removing Markers 2 through 5 as you encounter them, and moving Marker 6 4 sts to the end of Chart 3. K13 (17, 21).

Continue to follow Chart 3-Right as established between the markers, through Row 17 (17, 20).

Heel Flap

Starting at Marker 1, follow Row 21 (21, 25) of Chart 4 across the next 10 sts as follows: K1TBL, P4, K2, Sl1, K1, Sl1. K1. Turn.

Next Row (WS): Sl1, follow Row 22 (22, 26) of Chart 4 to Marker 1 as established, P13 (17, 21) to Marker 6, work Row 1 (1, 5) of Chart 4 across the next 10 sts as follows: P1TBL, K4, P5. P1. Turn. Put remaining sts on a holder and work these 35 (39, 43) sts back and forth for the heel flap.

Note: The two bands running down either side of the heel flap are slightly out-of-sync, and you have to keep track of the appropriate row for each DNA strand separately. This difference will be evened up when the heel is turned.

Next Row: Sl1, follow Row 2 (2, 6) of Chart 4 across the next 10 sts as follows: K1, Sl1, K1, K5, K1TBL. K1, [Sl1, K1] 6x (8x, 10x), follow Row 23 (23, 27) of Chart 4 as established, K1.

Continue the heel flap as established, slipping first st of every row, working Chart 4 across the two bands as appropriate (and repeating Rows 1-40 as necessary) and working the slip-stitch pattern as established in the panel between the bands, until the heel flap measures 2.5", ending with a WS row.

Turn Heel

Sl1, work appropriate row of Chart, remove Marker 6, K11 (13, 15), SSK, K1, turn. 1 st dec.

Next Row (WS): Sl1, P10, P2tog, P1, turn. 1 st dec.
Next Row (RS): Sl1, K11, SSK, K1, turn. 1 st dec.
Next Row: Sl1, P12, P2tog, P1, turn. 1 st dec.
Next Row: Sl1, K13, SSK, K1, turn. 1 st dec.

Continue in this manner, working one additional st each row, until all heel flap sts are incorporated, ending with a WS row. (Remove Marker 1 when you reach it.) Turn. 23 (25, 27) sts.

Gusset

K across 23 (25, 27) heel sts, then PU and K one st for each slipped st along the side of the heel flap. PM(1). Work across instep as follows: work Row 28 (1, 1) of Chart 2 across the first 10 sts (band A), PM(2), K1 (3, 5), PM(3), work Row 16 of Chart 1 across the next 14 sts (front strand), PM(4), K1 (3, 5), PM(5), work Row 13 (16, 16) of Chart 2 across the final 10 sts (band B), PM(6). PU and K one st for each slipped st along the next edge of the heel flap.

Next Rnd: K across heel sts, then KTBL sts along the side of the heel flap (gusset sts) until 2 gusset sts remain, K2tog, SM(1). Work across instep as follows: work Row 29 (29, 2) of Chart 2 across band A, SM(2), K 1 (3, 5), SM(3), work Row 17 of Chart 1 across the front strand, SM(4), K1 (3, 5), SM(5), work Row 14 (14, 17) of Chart 2 across band B. SM(6), SSK first 2 gusset sts, KTBL remaining gusset sts.

Next Rnd: K across heel and gusset sts, work across instep as established, K across gusset sts.

Next Rnd: K across heel sts, K to final 2 gusset sts, K2tog, work across instep as established, SSK first 2 gusset sts, K remaining gusset sts.

Rep these last 2 rnds until 71 (79, 87) sts remain: 36 (40, 44) sts across instep and 35 (39, 43) sts in gusset and heel sts combined.

Foot

Work all sts as established until foot measures 1.75 (2, 2.25)" less from back of heel than total length desired. Start of rnd is now located at mid-point of sole sts. Note that there are an odd number of sole sts; where exactly you put the new start of rnd isn't important as long as it's somewhere near the middle st.

Toe Decreases

Setup Rnd: K sole sts, SM(1), work the appropriate row of Chart 2 across band A, remove Marker 2, K1 (3, 5), remove Marker 3, work the appropriate row of Chart 1 across the front strand and dec one st in the strand, remove Marker 4, K1 (3, 5), remove Marker 5, work the appropriate row of Chart 2 across band B, SM6, K sole sts. 70 (78, 86) sts.

Next Rnd: *K to 3 sts before M, K2tog, K1, SM, K1, SSK, rep from * once more, K to end of rnd. 4 sts dec.

Next Rnd: K.

Rep these last 2 rnds until 26 (26, 30) sts remain, ending with a dec rnd. K across remaining sole sts. Break yarn. Use Kitchener stitch to graft toe closed.

Finishing

Weave in ends, wash and block to diagram.

Chart 1

14	13	12	11	10	9	8	7	6	5	4	3	2	1	
B	●	B				⧖B	⟋			B		●	B	30
B	●	B			⧖B	⟋				⟋	⧗B	●	B	29
B	●	⟋	⧗B	⧖B	⟋	●	●	●	●	B	●	B	28
B	●	●	B⧖	⟋						B	●	B	27
B	●	●	B	B						B	●	B	26
B	●	B⧖	⟋	⟋	⧗·	●	●	●	●	B	●	B	25
B	●	B			⟋	B⧗			⧖B	⟋	●	B	24
B	●	B				⟋	B⧗		B	●	●	B	23
B	●	B	●	●	●	●	⟋	⧗·	⧖B	⟋	●	●	B	22
B	●	B					B⧖	⟋		●	●	B	21
B	●	⟋	B⧗			⧖B	⟋	⟋	B⧗	●	●	B	20
B	●	●	B	●	●	⧖B	⟋	●	●	B	●	●	B	19
B	●	●	⟋	B⧗	⟋	B⧗	⟋	⟋	B⧗	●	●	B	18
B	●	●	●	B⧖	⟋			B	●	B	17
B	●	●	⧖B	⟋	⟋	⧗·	●	●	●	B	●	B	16
B	●	●	B		⟋	B⧗		B	●	B	15
B	●	⧖B	⟋	⟋	B⧗		B	●	B	14
B	●	B	●	●	●	●	⟋	⧗·	⧖B	⟋	●	B	13
B	●	B			B⧖	⟋	●	●	B	12
B	●	B			B	B	●	●	B	11
B	●	B	●	●	●	●	⧖B	⟋	⟋	B⧗	●	B	10
B	●	⟋	B⧗	⟋	B⧗		B	●	B	9
B	●	●	B	⟋	B⧗		B	●	B	8
B	●	●	⟋	B⧗	⧖B	⟋	●	●	●	B	●	B	7
B	●	●	B⧖	⟋		B	●	B	6
B	●	●	⧖B	⟋	⟋	B⧗	⟋	B⧗	●	B	5
B	●	●	B	●	●	⟋	⧗·	●	●	B	●	B	4
B	●	⧖B	⟋	⟋	B⧗	⟋	B⧗	●	B	3
B	●	B	B⧖	⟋	●	●	●	B	2
B	●	B	●	●	●	●	⧖B	⟋	⟋	B⧗	●	B	1

Legend

K
RS: Knit stitch
WS: Purl stitch

P
RS: Purl stitch
WS: Knit stitch

knit tbl
RS: Knit stitch through back loop
WS: Purl stitch through back loop

On Chart 4
To maintain continuity across the heel flap, on RS rows work [sl1, k1] or [k1, sl1] as appropriate across these sts.

C2Bk
RS: sl1 to CN, hold in back. k1tbl. k1 from CN.
WS: sl1 to CN, hold in back. p1. p1tbl from CN.

C2Fk
RS: sl1 to CN, hold in front. k1. k1tbl from CN.
WS: sl1 to CN, hold in front. p1tbl. p1 from CN.

C2Bt
RS: sl1 to CN, hold in back. k1tbl. k1tbl from CN.

C2Ft
RS: sl1 to CN, hold in front. k1tbl. k1tbl from CN.

C2Bp
RS: sl1 to CN, hold in back. k1tbl. p1 from CN.
WS: sl1 to CN, hold in back. k1. p1tbl from CN.

C2Fp
RS: sl1 to CN, hold in front. p1. k1tbl from CN.
WS: sl1 to CN, hold in front. p1tbl. k1 from CN.

Purled Left Twist
sl1 to CN and hold in front. p1, p1 from CN.

Chart 2

10	9	8	7	6	5	4	3	2	1	
B										30
B										29
⋋	B•	●	●	●						28
	B									27
⋋	B⋌									26
		⋋	B•	●	●					25
		⋋	B⋌							24
			⋋	B⋌						23
				⋋	B•					22
				⋋	B⋌					21
					⋋	B⋌				20
				●	●	●	B			19
						⋋	B⋌			18
								B		17
				●	●	●	●	B		16
								B		15
								B		14
				●	●	●	•⋌B	⋋		13
						⋌B	⋋			12
							B			11
				●	●	•⋌B	⋋			10
					⋌B	⋋				9
				⋌B	⋋					8
			•⋌B	⋋						7
		⋌B	⋋							6
	⋌B	⋋								5
	B	●	●	●						4
⋌B	⋋									3
B										2
B	●	●	●	●						1

Chart 3 - Left (7.75")

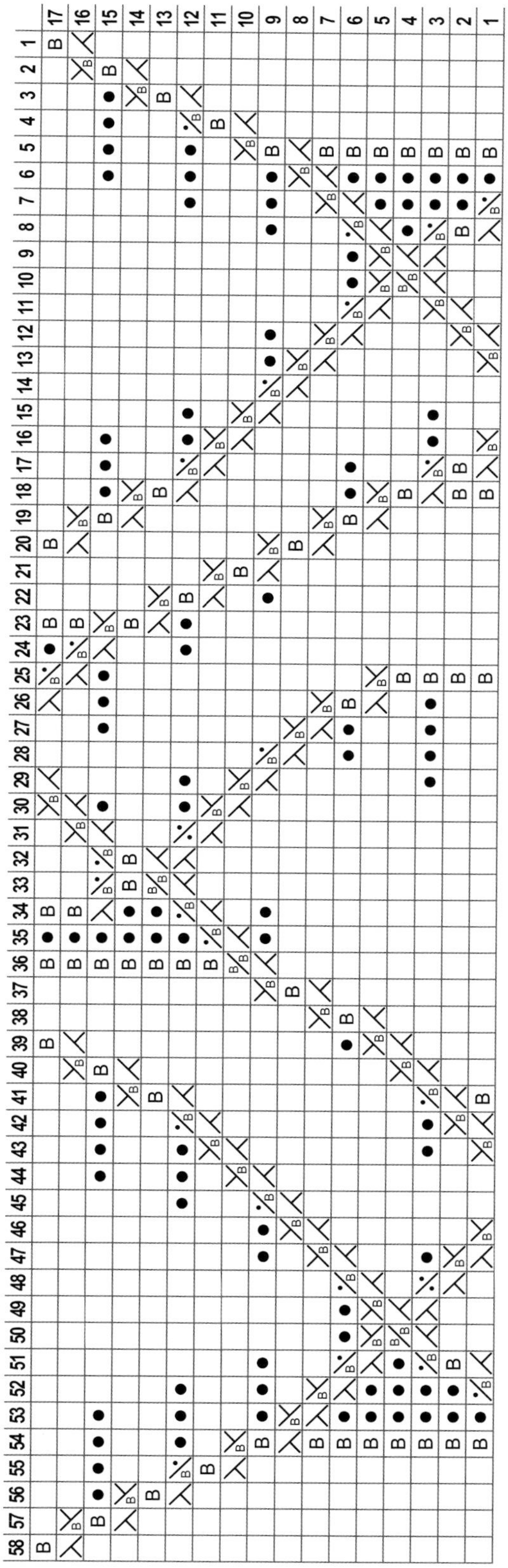

Chart 3 - Right (7.75")

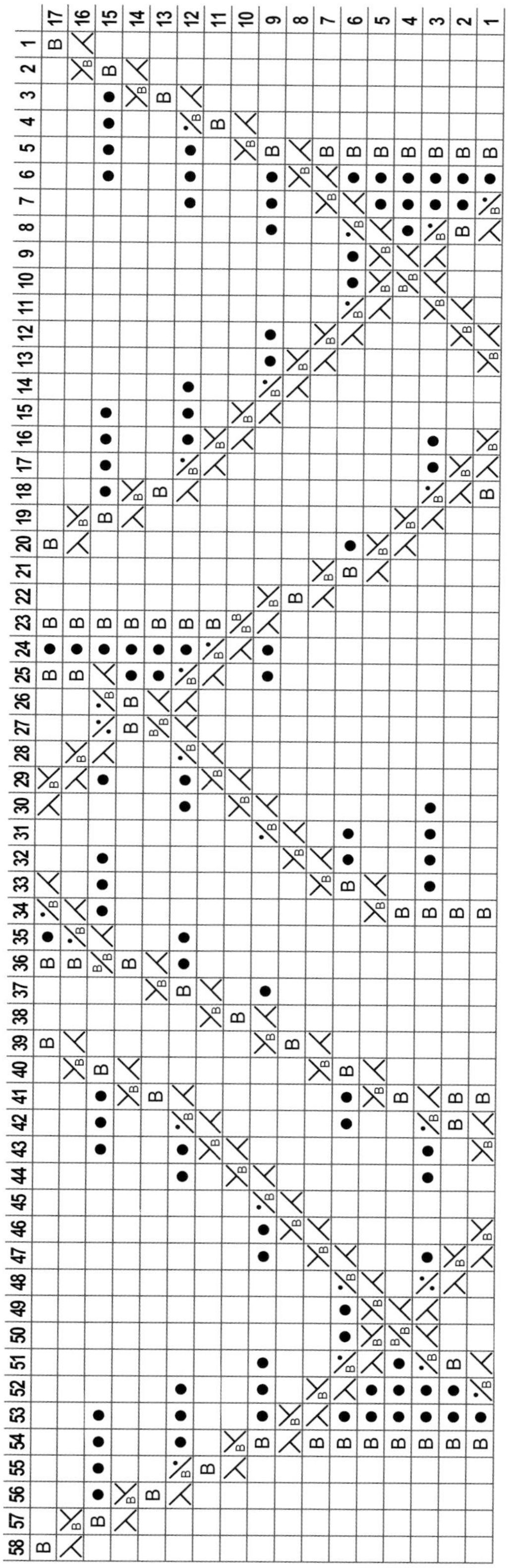

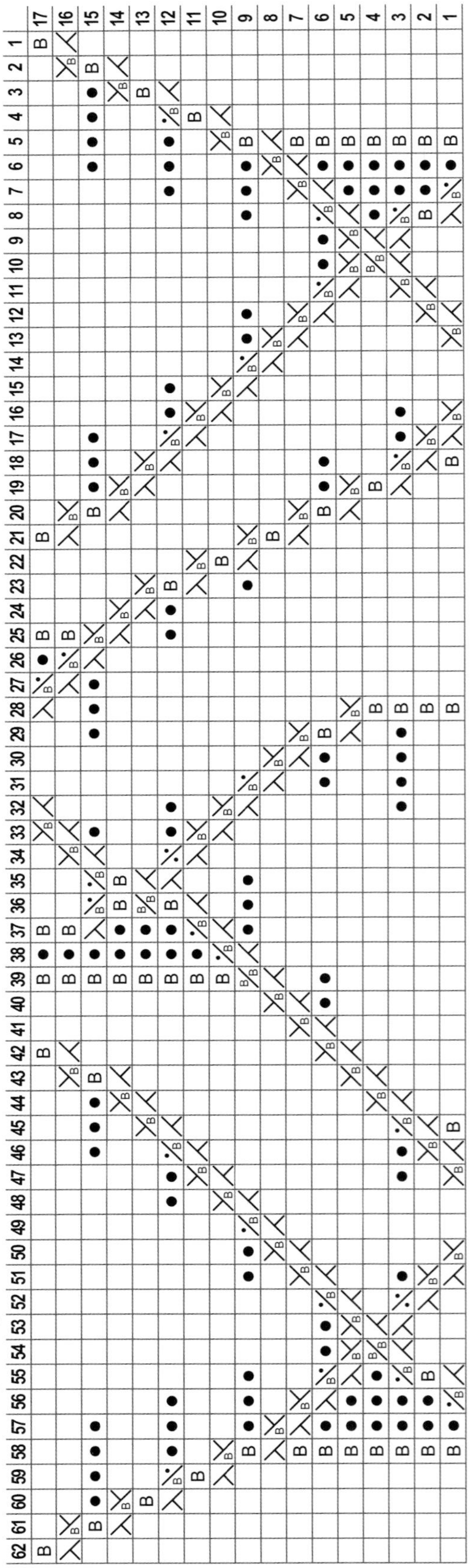

Chart 3 - Left (8.75")

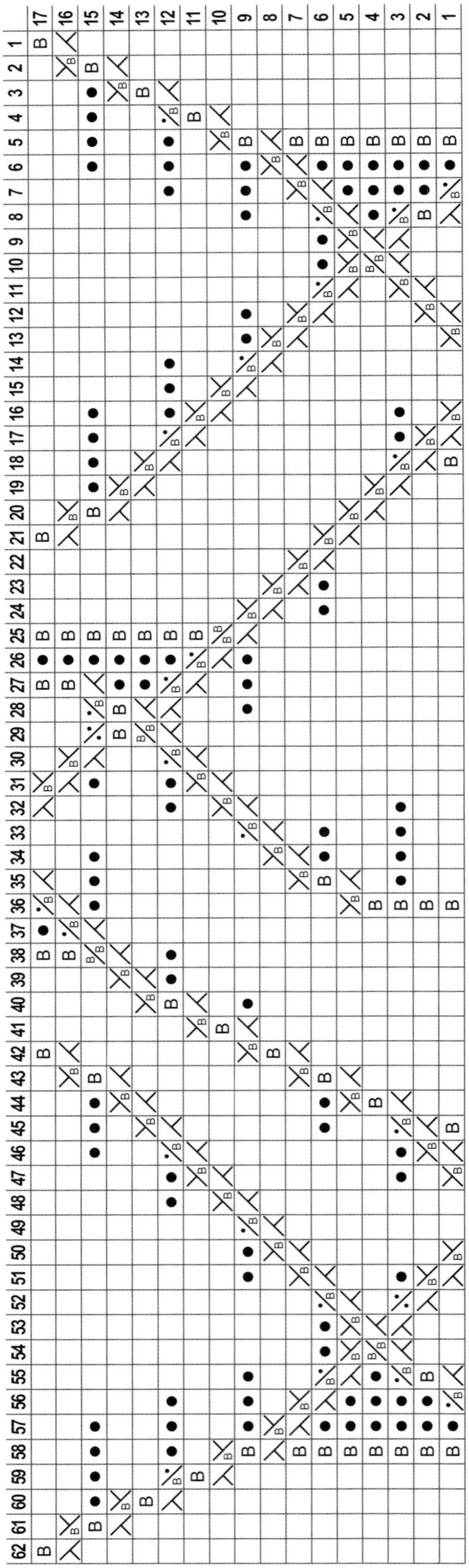

Chart 3 - Right (8.75")

Chart 3 - Left (9.75")

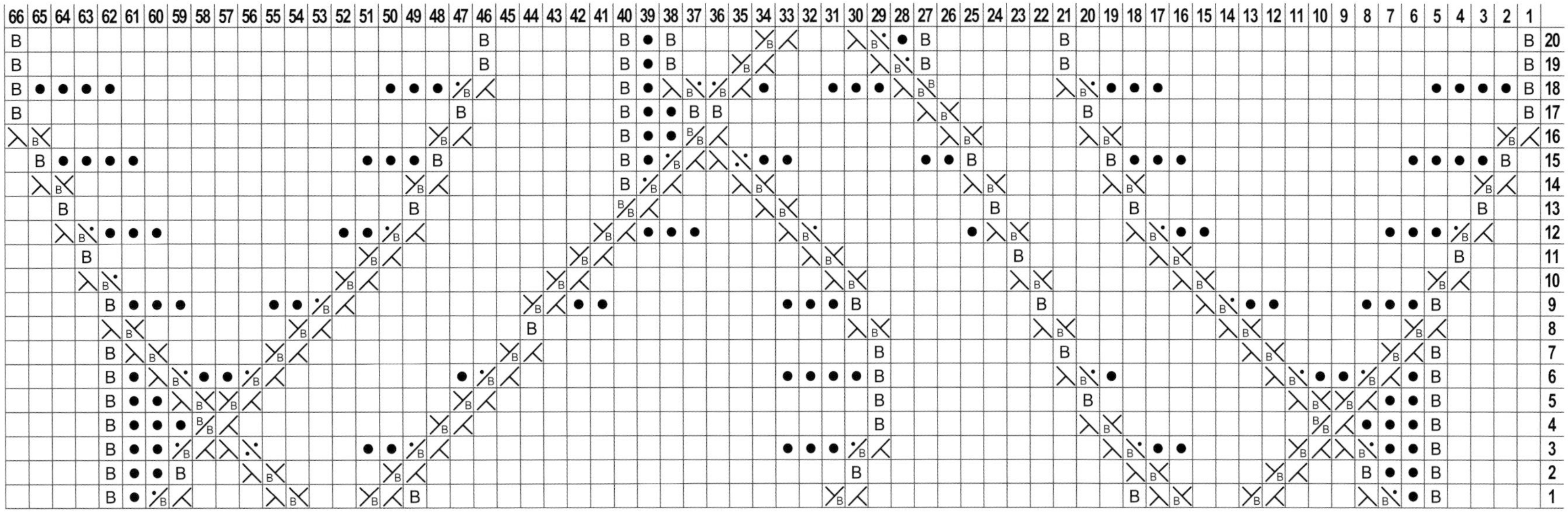

Chart 3 - Right (9.75")

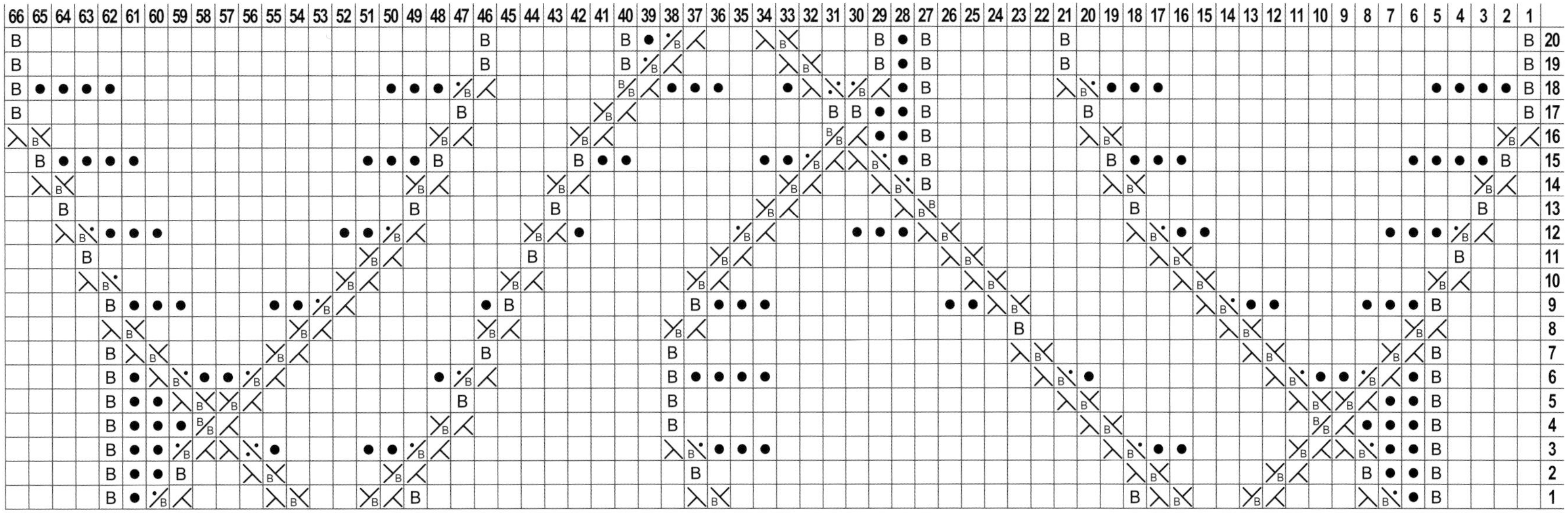

Chart 4

Row	10	9	8	7	6	5	4	3	2	1	Row
40		B					■	■	■	■	
		B					■	■	■	■	39
38		⤬	⤬ᵦ				■	■	■	■	
			B	●	●	●	■	■	■	■	37
36			⤬	⤬ᵦ			■	■			
	■			⤬	⤬ᵦ		■	■			35
34	■	■			⤬	⤬ᵦ		■			
	■	■	■		⤬	⤬ᵦ•				■	33
32	■	■	■			⤬	⤬ᵦ				
	■	■	■				B				31
30	■	■	■				⤬	⤬ᵦ			
	■	■	■		●	●	●	B			29
28	■	■	■					B			
	■	■	■					⤬	⤬ᵦ		27
26	■	■	■						B		
	■	■	■		●	●	●	●	B		25
24	■	■	■						B		
	■	■	■						B		23
22	■	■	■						B		
	■	■	■		●	●	●	⤬ᵦ	⤬		21
20	■	■	■					B			
	■	■	■					B			19
18	■	■	■				⤬ᵦ	⤬			
	■	■	■	■	●	●	●	B			17
16	■	■	■	■		⤬ᵦ	⤬				
	■	■	■		⤬ᵦ	⤬				■	15
14	■	■	■		⤬ᵦ	⤬			■	■	
	■	■		⤬ᵦ•	⤬			■	■	■	13
12	■		⤬ᵦ	⤬			■	■	■	■	
			B				■	■	■	■	11
10		⤬ᵦ	⤬				■	■	■	■	
		B	●	●	●		■	■	■	■	9
8		B					■	■	■	■	
	⤬ᵦ	⤬					■	■	■	■	7
6	B						■	■	■	■	
	B	●	●	●	●		■	■	■	■	5
4	B						■	■	■	■	
	B						■	■	■	■	3
2	B						■	■	■	■	
	⤬	⤬ᵦ•					■	■	■	■	1

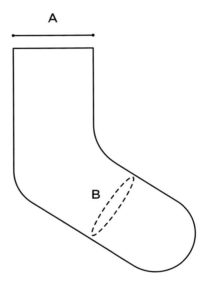

A Leg Circumference: 7.75 (8.75, 9.75)"
B Foot Circumference: 7.75 (8.75, 9.75)"

Left Sock

Left Side

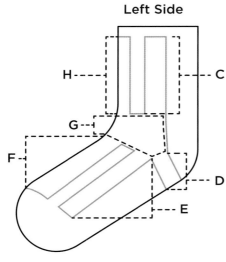

Right Side

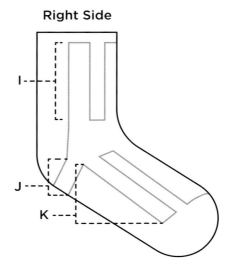

C Band B: Chart 1, Rows 1-30, then Rows 1-13.

D Heel Flap: Chart 4, Rows 22 (22-26)-40, then repeat Rows 1-40 as necessary.

E Band B: Chart 2, Row 13 (16, 16), then Rows 14 (14, 17)-30, then repeat Rows 1-30 as necessary.

F Front Strand: Chart 1, Rows 16-30, then repeat Rows 1-30 as necessary.

G Denaturing the Helix: Chart 3-L, Rows 1-17 (17, 20).

H Front Strand: Chart 2, Rows 1-30, then Rows 1-13. (Size 9.75″ only: Rows 28-30, then Rows 1-30, then Rows 1-10).

I Band A: Chart 1, Rows 16-30, then Rows 1-28.

J Heel Flap: Chart 4, Rows 21 (21, 25)-40, then repeat Rows 1-40 as necessary.

K Band A: Chart 2, Row 28 (1, 1), then Rows 29 (29, 2)-30, then repeat Rows 1-30 as necessary.

Right Sock

Left Side

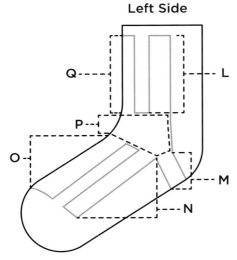

Right Side

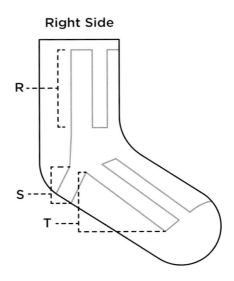

L Band B: Chart 1, Rows 1-30, then Rows 1-13.

M Heel Flap: Chart 4, Rows 22 (22-26)-40, then repeat Rows 1-40 as necessary.

N Band B: Chart 2, Row 13 (16, 16), then Rows 14 (14, 17)-30, then repeat Rows 1-30 as necessary.

O Front Strand: Chart 1, Rows 16-30, then repeat Rows 1-30 as necessary.

P Denaturing the Helix: Chart 3-R, Rows 1-17 (17, 20).

Q Front Strand: Chart 2 Rows 16 (16, 13)-30, then Rows 1-28 (28, 25).

R Band A: Chart 1, Rows 16-30, then Rows 1-28.

S Heel Flap: Chart 4, Rows 21 (21, 25)-40, then repeat Rows 1-40 as necessary.

T Band A: Chart 2, Row 28 (1, 1), then Rows 29 (29,2)-30, then repeat Rows 1-30 as necessary.

TRANSVERSAL SOCKS

Mone Dräger

FINISHED MEASUREMENTS

7 (8, 9)" leg circumference; 8 (9, 9.75)"
leg length including heel when knit as
given in the pattern; 7.5 (8.75, 10)" foot
length, adjustable for more length.

YARN

Knit Picks Hawthorne Tonal Hand Paint
(80% Superwash Fine Highland
Wool, 20% Polyamide (Nylon); 357
yards/100g): Astoria 27411, 1 skein.

NEEDLES

US 1 (2.5mm) DPNs or two 24" circular
needles for two circulars technique, or one
32" or longer circular needle for Magic
Loop technique, or size to obtain gauge.

NOTIONS

Stitch Markers
Cable Needle
Yarn Needle

GAUGE

32 sts and 42 rows = 4" in Transversal
Pattern in the rnd, blocked.
22 sts and 60 rows = 4" in Slipped St
Heel pattern, blocked.
32 sts and 42 rows = 4" in St st in the
rnd, blocked.

For pattern support, contact
mone.draeger@gmx.de

Notes:

The Transversal socks feature an interesting, architectural cable pattern. The pattern was inspired by the look of half-timbered houses with their wooden frames and filled panels between. The background pattern are segments in Stockinette stitch and reverse Stockinette stitch, alternating every couple of rounds, which get divided by diagonal cable lines. A classy pattern, suitable for women and men alike.

The socks are knitted from the cuff down, with heel flap and gusset. When working the charts in the round, follow each row from right to left, as a RS row.

C2over 1 left: Sl2 to CN, hold in front, K1, K2 from CN
C2 over 1 right: Sl1 to CN, hold in back, K2, K1 from CN
C2 over 1 right P: Sl1 to CN, hold in back, K2, P1 from CN
C2 over 2 left: Sl2 to CN, hold in front, K2, K2 from CN
C2 over 2 right: Sl2 to CN, hold in back, K2, K2 from CN

K2, P2 Rib (in the rnd over multiples of 4 sts)
Rnd 1: *K2, P2; rep from * to end.
Rep Rnd 1 for pattern.

Transversal Pattern (worked in the rnd over 14 [16, 18] sts)
Size L 9" only:
Rnd 1: C2 over 1 left, K6, P6, C2 over 1 right P.
Rnd 2: K9, P6, K2, P1.

Size M 8" and L 9" only:
Rnd 3: K0 (1), C2 over 1 left, K5, P5, C2 over 1 right P, P0 (1).
Rnd 4: K8 (9), P5, K2, P1 (2).

All Sizes
Rnd 5: K0 (1, 2), C2 over 1 left, K4, P4, C2 over 1 right P, P0 (1, 2).
Rnd 6: K7 (8, 9), P4, K2, P1 (2, 3).
Rnd 7: K1 (2, 3), C2 over 1 left, K3, P3, C2 over 1 right P, P1 (2, 3).
Rnd 8: K7 (8, 9), P3, K2, P2 (3, 4).
Rnd 9: K2 (3, 4), C2 over 1 left, K2, P2, C2 over 1 right P, P2 (3, 4).
Rnd 10: K7 (8, 9), P2, K2, P3 (4, 5).
Rnd 11: K3 (4, 5), C2 over 1 left, K1, P1, C2 over 1 right P, P3 (4, 5).
Rnd 12: K7 (8, 9), P1, K2, P4 (5, 6).
Rnd 13: K4 (5, 6), C2 over 1 left, C2 over 1 right P, P4 (5, 6).
Rnd 14: K9 (10, 11), P5 (6, 7).
Rnd 15: P5 (6, 7), C2 over 2 right, K5 (6, 7).
Rnd 16: P5 (6, 7), K9 (10, 11).
Rnd 17: P4 (5, 6), C2 over 1 right P, C2 over 1 left, K4 (5, 6).
Rnd 18: P4 (5, 6), K2, P1, K7 (8, 9).
Rnd 19: P3 (4, 5), C2 over 1 right P, P1, K1, C2 over 1 left, K3 (4, 5).
Rnd 20: P3 (4, 5), K2, P2, K7 (8, 9).
Rnd 21: P2 (3, 4), C2 over 1 right P, P2, K2, C2 over 1 left, K2 (3, 4).
Rnd 22: P2 (3, 4), K2, P3, K7 (8, 9).
Rnd 23: P1 (2, 3), C2 over 1 right P, P3, K3, C2 over 1 left, K1 (2, 3).
Rnd 24: P1 (2, 3), K2, P4, K7 (8, 9).
Rnd 25: P0 (1, 2), C2 over 1 right P, P4, K4, C2 over 1 left, K0 (1, 2).
Rnd 26: P0 (1, 2), K2, P5, K7 (8, 9).

Size M 8" and L 9" only:
Rnd 27: P0 (1), C2 over 1 right P, P5, K5, C2 over 1 left, K0 (1).
Rnd 28: P0 (1), K2, P6, K8 (9).

Size L 9" only:
Rnd 29: C2 over 1 right P, P6, K6, C2 over 1 left.
Rnd 30: K2, P7, K9.

Transversal Foot Pattern (in the rnd over 14 [16, 18] sts)

Rnd 1: P4 (5, 6), C2 over 1 right, C2 over 1 left, K4 (5, 6).
Rnd 2: P4 (5, 6), K10 (11, 12).
Rnd 3: P3 (4, 5), C2 over 1 right, K2, C2 over 1 left, K3 (4, 5).
Rnd 4: P3 (4, 5), K11 (12, 13).
Rnd 5: P2 (3, 4), C2 over 1 right, K4, C2 over 1 left, K2 (3, 4).
Rnd 6: P2 (3, 4), K12 (13, 14).
Rnd 7: P1 (2, 3), C2 over 1 right, K6, C2 over 1 left, K1 (2, 3).
Rnd 8: P1 (2, 3), K13, (14, 15).
Rnd 9: P0 (1, 2), C2 over 1 right, K8, C2 over 1 left, K0 (1, 2).
Rnd 10: P0 (1, 2), K14 (15, 16).

Size M 8" and L 9" only:
Rnd 11: P0 (1), C2 over 1 right, K10, C2 over 1 left, K0 (1).
Rnd 12: P0 (1), K16 (17).

Size L 9" only:
Rnd 13: C2 over 1 right, K12, C2 over 1 left.
Rnd 14: Knit.

Kitchener Stitch (grafting)
With an equal number of sts on two needles, thread end of working yarn through yarn needle. Hold needles parallel with RS facing and both needles pointing to the right. Perform Step 2 on the first front st, and then Step 4 on the first back st, and then continue with instructions below.
Step 1: Pull yarn needle K-wise though front st and drop st from knitting needle.
Step 2: Pull yarn needle P-wise through next front st, leave st on knitting needle.
Step 3: Pull yarn needle P-wise through first back st and drop st from knitting needle.
Step 4: Pull yarn needle K-wise through next back st, leave st on knitting needle.

Rep Steps 1 – 4 until all sts have been grafted.

DIRECTIONS

Cuff

Loosely CO 56 (64, 72) sts. Join to work in the rnd and PM, being careful not to twist sts.
Work in K2, P2 Rib for 16 rnds.

Leg

Set-up Rnd 1: *C2 over 2 left, K5 (6, 7), P5 (6, 7), rep from * to end of rnd.
Set-up Rnd 2: Remove M, K2, PM for new beginning of rnd *K7 (8, 9), P7 (8, 9); rep from * to end of rnd.
Work Rnds 5-26 (3-28, 1-30) of Transversal Pattern.
Intermediate Rnd 1: Sl2, *K5 (6, 7), P5 (6, 7), C2 over 2 left; rep from * 3 more times, using the first 2 sts of the next rnd to complete final cable.
Intermediate Rnd 2: K7 (8, 9), *P5 (6, 7), K9 (10, 11); rep from * 2 more times, P5 (6, 7), K2.
Work Rnds 5-26 (3-28, 1-30) of Transversal Pattern.

Heel Flap

Set-up Rnd 1: Sl2, [K5 (6, 7), P5 (6, 7), C2 over 2 left] twice, [K10 (12, 14), C2 over 2 left] twice, using the first 2 sts of the next rnd to complete final cable.
Set-up Rnd 2: K5 (6, 7), P5 (6, 7), K9 (10, 11), P5 (6, 7); K to end of rnd, turn.
The heel flap is worked back and forth over the 28 (32, 36) sts just worked, starting with a WS row. Keep remaining 28 (32, 36) sts on hold for instep.
Row 1 (WS): K1, *Sl1, P1; rep from * 12 (14, 16) more times, K1.
Row 2 (RS): Knit.
Row 3: K1, *P1, Sl1; rep from * 12 (14, 16) more times, K1.
Row 4: Knit.
Rep Rows 1-4 six (six, seven) more times.
Size M 8" only: Rep Rows 1-2 once more.

Turn Heel

Short- Row 1 (WS): Sl1 WYIF, P16 (18, 20), P2tog, P1, turn.
Short- Row 2 (RS): Sl1 WYIB, K7, SSK, K1, turn.
Short-Row 3: Sl1 WYIF, P to 1 st before the gap, P2tog, P1, turn.
Short-Row 4: Sl1 WYIB, K to 1 st before the gap, SSK, K1, turn.
Rep Short-Rows 3-4 three (four, five) more times. Do not turn after last row. 18 (20, 22) heel sts.

Gusset

Set-up Rnd 1: PU and K14 (15, 16) sts along the edge of the heel flap, PM for beginning of rnd.
Set-up Rnd 2: Work instep sts in Transversal Pattern as established, PM, PU and K14 (15, 16) sts along the edge of the heel flap, K to end. 74 (82, 90) sts; 28 (32, 36) on instep, 46 (50, 54) on sole.
Rnd 1: Work to M in Transversal Pattern, SM, K1, SSK, K to last 3 sts, K2tog, K1. 2 sts dec.
Rnd 2: Work to M in Transversal Pattern, K to end.
Rep Rnds 1-2 eight more times. 56 (64, 72) sts; 28 (32, 36) each on instep and sole.

Foot

Cont in established pattern, working all instep sts in Transversal Pattern and knitting all sole sts, until Rnds 5-26 (3-28, 1-30) of Transversal pattern have been worked.
Intermediate Rnd 1: K7 (8, 9), P5 (6, 7), C2 over 2 left, K5 (6, 7), P5 (6, 7), K to end.
Intermediate Rnd 2: K7 (8, 9), P5 (6, 7), K9 (10, 11), P5 (6, 7), K to end.
Cont in established pattern, working instep sts in Transversal Pattern and knitting all sole sts, until Rnds 5-16 (3-16, 1-16) of Transversal Pattern have been worked.

Next Rnd: Work to M from Transversal Foot Pattern, K to end.
Continue as established in last rnd, until Rnds 1-10 (1-12, 1-14) of the Transversal Foot pattern have been worked

Next Rnd: K 12 (14, 16), C2 over 2 left, K to end.
Work even in St st, i.e. K all sts, for 8 rnds or until foot measures 1.5 (1.75, 2.25)" less than the desired foot length.

Toe

Rnd 1: *K1, SSK, K to 3 sts before M, K2tog, K1; rep from * once. 4 sts dec.
Rnd 2: Knit.
Rep Rnds 1-2 four (six, eight) more times. 36 sts.
Rep Rnd 1 five more times. 16 sts.
Cut yarn, leaving an 18" tail. Use the yarn needle and tail and graft the instep sts to the sole sts, using Kitchener Stitch.

Finishing

Weave in ends, wash and block lightly.

Transversal Chart

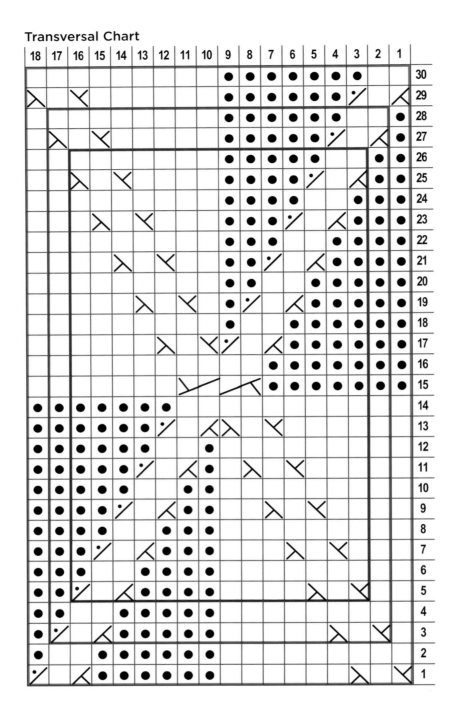

Legend

⬜ **K** Knit stitch	⬜ **Size S 7"**	c2 over 1 left — sl2 to CN, hold in front. k1, k2 from CN.
⬛ **P** Purl stitch	⬜ **Size M 8"**	c2 over 1 right — sl1 to CN, hold in back. k2, k1 from CN.
	⬜ **Size L 9"**	c2 over 1 right P — sl2 to CN, hold in back. k2, p1 from CN.
		c2 over 2 right — sl2 to CN, hold in back. k2, k2 from CN.

Transversal Foot Chart

18	17	16	15	14	13	12	11	10	9	8	7	6	5	4	3	2	1	
																		14
⟍		⟍													Y		⟍	13
																	●	12
		⟍		⟍											Y	⟍	●	11
																●	●	10
			⟍		⟍								Y	⟍	⟍	●	●	9
														●	●	●	●	8
				⟍		⟍					Y		⟍	●	●	●	●	7
												●	●	●	●	●	●	6
				⟍		⟍				Y		⟍	●	●	●	●	●	5
											●	●	●	●	●	●	●	4
					⟍		⟍		Y		⟍	●	●	●	●	●	●	3
										●	●	●	●	●	●	●	●	2
						⟍		⟍Y	⟍	●	●	●	●	●	●	●	●	1

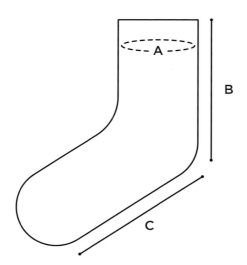

A 7 (8, 9)"
B 8 (9, 9.75)"
C 7.5 (8.75, 10)", adjustable for more length.

TWISTED RIB CABLEMANIA

by Tiam Safari

FINISHED MEASUREMENTS

7 (8, 9)" foot circumference; to fit women's sock sizes 7-9 (9-11, 10-12).

YARN

Knit Picks Capretta
(80% Fine Merino Wool, 10% Cashmere, 10% Nylon; 230 yards/50g): Turmeric 25948, 2 balls.

NEEDLES

US 2 (2.75mm) two 24" circular needles for Two Circular technique, or size to obtain gauge.

NOTIONS

Yarn Needle
Stitch Markers (optional)
Cable Needle
Scrap Yarn or Stitch Holder

GAUGE

30 sts and 40 rows = 4" in St st in the rnd, blocked gently.
36 sts and 36 rows = 4" over Chart C in the rnd, blocked gently.

For pattern support, contact
info@knitsafari.com

Notes:

These socks are a testament to the beauty of twisted ribs and cables, with a basic toe and heel construction to allow the motif to take center stage, while allowing seasoned sock knitters to substitute in their favorite technique.

These socks are knitted toe-up, and can be knitted two-at-a-time for the perfect matching pair.

The chart rows are followed from right to left, and read as RS rows.

Judy's Magic Cast On tutorial can be found here: http://tutorials.knitpicks.com/judys-magic-cast-on/.

Wrap and Turn (W&T): Tutorial on Knit Picks website can be found here: http://tutorials.knitpicks.com/wptutorials/short-rows-wrap-and-turn-or-wt/.

DIRECTIONS

Toe

CO 13 (16, 18) sts using any invisible CO technique, to each of two needles. 26 (32, 36) sts. Judy's Magic Cast-On is a good option.

Rnd 1: K all sts.

Rnd 2: Needle 1: *K1, M1R, K to last st, M1L, K1; rep from * on Needle 2. 4 sts inc. 30 (36, 40) sts.

Rep Rnds 1-2 five (five, six) more times. 25 (28, 32) sts each needle, 50 (56, 64) sts total.

Arrange your sts as follows: Needle 1, top of foot: 24 (28, 32) sts. Needle 2, sole of foot: 26 (28, 32) sts.

Foot

Needle 1: K0 (1, 1), P0 (1, 1), K0 (0, 1), P0 (0, 1), work Twisted Rib Stitch Pattern Chart A to last 0 (2, 4) sts, P0 (1, 1), K0 (1, 1), P0 (0, 1), K0 (0, 1). Needle 2: K all sts.

Keeping first 0 (2, 4) and last 0 (2, 4) sts as established, continue working Chart A until 2 reps of Rnds 1-6 have been worked across Needle 1, then work Twisted Rib Stitch Pattern Chart B on Needle 1 until 9 reps have been completed. Finish at the end of Needle 2.

Bottom of Heel

Work back and forth on Needle 2 only, to work the heel of the sock.

Row 1 (WS): P25 (27, 31), W&T.

Row 2 (RS): K24 (26, 30), W&T.

Rep Rows 1-2 working one fewer st on each side, until 8 unwrapped sts remain in the center of the needles.

Back of Heel

Row 1 (WS): P across to wrapped st, PU the wrap first and P it with the st that is wrapped.

Row 2 (RS): K across to wrapped st, PU the wrap first and K it with the st that is wrapped.

Rep Rows 1-2 until all wrapped sts have been worked, finishing on a RS row.

Leg

You will now continue to work in the rnd.

Rnd 1: Needle 1: *M1, K0 (1, 1), P0 (1, 1), K0 (0, 1), P0 (0, 1), work Chart B starting at Rnd 1, P0 (1, 1), K0 (1, 1), P0 (0, 1), K0 (0, 1); rep from * for Needle 2. Needle 1: 25 (29, 33) sts, Needle 2: 27 (29, 33) sts, 52 (58, 66) sts total.

Rnd 2: Needle 1: *P1, K0 (1, 1), P0 (1, 1), K0 (0, 1), P0 (0, 1), continue working Chart B, P0 (1, 1), K0 (1, 1), P0 (0, 1), K0 (0, 1); rep from * for Needle 2.

Keeping first 1 (3, 5) and last 1 (3, 5) sts as established, continue working Chart B until 5 reps have been worked across Needle 1 and Needle 2.

Begin Chart C: Needle 1: *Work first 1 (3, 5) sts as established, work Row 1 of Twisted Rib Cable Pattern Chart C, work to end as established; rep from * for Needle 2. 52 (58, 66) sts. Cont working as established until the end of Chart C.

Next Rnd: Cont to rep Rnd 22 of Chart C for 22 (24, 26) more rnds. BO loosely, or try Jeny's Surprisingly Stretchy Bind-Off.

Finishing

Weave in ends, wash and block gently to dimensions.

Twisted Rib Stitch Pattern Chart A

24	23	22	21	20	19	18	17	16	15	14	13	12	11	10	9	8	7	6	5	4	3	2	1	
B	●	B	●		O	B	●	B	●	╱	●	●	●	╲	●	B	●	B	O		●	B	●	6
B	●	B	●	O	B	●	B	●	╱	B	●	●	B	╲	●	B	●	B	O	●	B	●	B	5
B	●		O	B	●	B	●	╱	●	B	●	●	B	●	╲	●	B	●	B	O		●	B	4
B	●	O	B	●	B	●	╱	●	●	B	●	●	B	●	●	╲	●	B	●	B	O	●	B	3
	O	B	●	B	●	╱	B	●	●	B	●	●	B	●	●	B	╲	●	B	●	B	O		2
O	B	●	B	●	╱	●	●	B	●	●	B	●	●	B	●	●	B	╲	●	B	●	B	O	1
	●		●		●	●		●	●		●	●		●	●		●	●		●		●		Setup Row

Twisted Rib Stitch Pattern Chart B

24	23	22	21	20	19	18	17	16	15	14	13	12	11	10	9	8	7	6	5	4	3	2	1	
╲	●	B	●	B	O		●	B	●	B	●	●	B	●	B	●		O	B	●	B	●	╱	6
B	╲	●	B	●	B	O		●	B	●	B	●	●	B	●	B	●	O	B	●	B	●	╱	5
B	●	╲	●	B	●	B	O		●	B	●	●	B	●		O	B	●	B	●	╱	●	B	4
B	●	B	╲	●	B	●	B	O		●	B	●	●	B	●	O	B	●	B	●	╱	B	●	3
B	●	B	●	╲	●	B	●	B	O		●	●		O	B	●	B	●	╱	●	B	●	B	2
B	●	B	●	B	╲	●	B	●	B	O	●	●	O	B	●	B	●	╱	B	●	B	●	B	1

Legend

☐	**K** — Knit stitch
●	**P** — Purl stitch
O	**yo** — Yarn Over
B	**knit tbl** — Knit stitch through back loop.
╲	**k2tog tbl** — Knit two stitches together in back loops as one
╱	**sl1, sl1t, k2tog** — Slip 1. Slip 1 twisted, then k2tog
☐	**Pattern Repeat**

c2 over 1 left P — sl2 to CN, hold in front. p1, k2 from CN.

c2 over 1 right P — sl2 to CN, hold in back. k2, p1 from CN.

k1 tbl, p2, k1 tbl — Leave yarn at back and slip 4 worked sts to LH needle. Bring yarn to front between needles and slip 4 worked sts to RH needle. Bring yarn to back between needles, ready to work the next st.

Twisted Rib Stitch Pattern Chart C

24	23	22	21	20	19	18	17	16	15	14	13	12	11	10	9	8	7	6	5	4	3	2	1	
●	B	●	●	B	●	●	B	●	●	B	●	●	B	●	●	B	●	●	B	●	●	B	●	22
●	B	●	●	B	●	●	B	●	●	B	●	●	B	●	●	B	●	●	B	●	●	B	●	21
●	B	●	●	B	●	●	B	●	●	B	●	●	B	●	●	B	●	●	B	●	●	B	●	20
●	B	●	●	B	●	●	B	●	●	B	●	●	B	●	●	B	●	●	B	●	●	B	●	19
●	B	●	●	B	●	●	B	●	●	B—●—●—B			B	●	●	B	●	●	B	●	●	B	●	18
●	B	●	●	B	●	●	B	●	●	B	●	●	B	●	●	B	●	●	B	●	●	B	●	17
●	B	●	●	B	●	●	B—●—●—B			●	●	B—●—●—B			B	●	●	B	●	●	B	●	16
●	B	●	●	B	●	●	B	●	●	B	●	●	B	●	●	B	●	●	B	●	●	B	●	15
●	B	●	●	B—●—●—B			●	●	B—●—●—B			●	●	B—●—●—B			●	●	B	●	14
●	B	●	●	B	●	●	B	●	●	B	●	●	B	●	●	B	●	●	B	●	●	B	●	13
●	B—●—●—B			●	●	B—●—●—B			●	●	B—●—●—B			●	●	B—●—●—B			●	12
●	B	●	●	B	●	●	B	●	●	B	●	●	B	●	●	B	●	●	B	●	●	B	●	11
●	B	●	●	B—●—●—B			●	●	B—●—●—B			●	●	B—●—●—B			●	●	B	●	10
●	B	●	●	B	●	●	B	●	●	B	●	●	B	●	●	B	●	●	B	●	●	B	●	9
●	B	●	●	B	●	●	B—●—●—B			●	●	B—●—●—B			●	●	B	●	●	B	●	8
●	B	●	●	B	●	●	B	●	●	B	●	●	B	●	●	B	●	●	B	●	●	B	●	7
●	B	●	●	B	●	●	B	●	●	B—●—●—B			●	●	B	●	●	B	●	●	B	●	6
●	B	●	●	B	●	●	B	●	●	B	●	●	B	●	●	B	●	●	B	●	●	B	●	5
●	B	●	●	B	●	●	B	●	●	B	●	●	B	●	●	B	●	●	B	●	●	B	●	4
●	B	●	●	B	●	●	B	●	●	B	●	●	B	●	●	B	●	●	B	●	●	B	●	3
●	B	●	●	B	●	●	B	●	●	B	●	●	B	●	●	B	●	●	B	●	●	B	●	2
╱		⟨	●	B	●	●	B	●	●	B	●	●	B	●	●	B	●	●	B	●	⟩		╲	1

Abbreviations

BO   bind off

BOR   beginning of round

cn   cable needle

CC   contrast color

CDD   Centered double dec

CO   cast on

cont   continue

dec   decrease(es)

DPN(s)   double pointed needle(s)

EOR   every other row

inc   increase

K   knit

K2tog   knit two sts together

KFB   knit into the front and back of stitch

K-wise   knitwise

LH   left hand

M   marker

M1   make one stitch

M1L   make one left-leaning stitch

M1R   make one right-leaning stitch

MC   main color

P   purl

P2tog   purl 2 sts together

PM   place marker

PFB   purl into the front and back of stitch

PSSO   pass slipped stitch over

PU   pick up

P-wise   purlwise

rep   repeat

Rev St st   reverse stockinette stitch

RH   right hand

rnd(s)   round(s)

RS   right side

Sk   skip

Sk2p   sl 1, k2tog, pass slipped stitch over k2tog: 2 sts dec

SKP   sl, k, psso: 1 st dec

SL   slip

SM   slip marker

SSK   sl, sl, k these 2 sts tog

SSP   sl, sl, p these 2 sts tog tbl

SSSK   sl, sl, sl, k these 3 sts tog

St st   stockinette stitch

sts   stitch(es)

TBL   through back loop

TFL   through front loop

tog   together

W&T   wrap & turn (see specific instructions in pattern)

WE   work even

WS   wrong side

WYIB   with yarn in back

WYIF   with yarn in front

YO   yarn over

Knit Picks yarn is both luxe and affordable—a seeming contradiction trounced! But it's not just about the pretty colors; we also care deeply about fiber quality and fair labor practices, leaving you with a gorgeously reliable product you'll turn to time and time again.

THIS COLLECTION FEATURES

Hawthorne Kettle Dye
Fingering Weight
80% Superwash Fine Highland Wool,
20% Polyamide (Nylon)

Hawthorne Multi
Fingering Weight
80% Superwash Fine Highland Wool,
20% Polyamide (Nylon)

Hawthorne Tonal
Fingering Weight
80% Superwash Fine Highland Wool,
20% Polyamide (Nylon)

Stroll Sock Yarn
Fingering Weight
75% Superwash Merino Wool,
25% Nylon

Stroll Tonal Sock Yarn
Fingering Weight
75% Superwash MerinoWool,
25% Nylon

Stroll Tweed Sock Yarn
Fingering Weight
65% Superwash Merino Wool,
25% Nylon, 10% Donegal

Capretta
Fingering Weight
80% Fine Merino Wool,
10% Cashmere, 10% Nylon

Gloss
Fingering Weight
70% Merino Wool,
30% Silk

View these beautiful yarns and more at www.Knit Picks.com